Reiki Healing First Degree
New Awakening System

**This Home Study Multimedia Course is all about
Healing Yourself, Family, Friends, Pets and Plants**

Home Study Multimedia Learning Material available for this Course
Course Book Manual, Reiki Music CD, Tutorial Audio Course CD
Free Healing Treatment Tutorials and Self Attunement Videos

"Welcome to your complete multimedia home study course.
I wish you every success in every area of your life"

Robert Bourne
Reiki Master Teacher

Naturally You
Publishing

United Kingdom

New Awakening Reiki Healing First Degree

Copyright © 2008 by Robert Bourne

ISBN 978-0-9561159-4-2

A catalogue of this publication is available from the British Library

Naturally You
Publishing

Published by Naturally You Publishing
All books and multimedia courses are distributed by Naturally You

Copyright © 2008 by Robert Bourne

For the latest information on
Spirituality, Healing and Sports Psychology please visit our website

www.naturallyyou.co.uk

'Naturally You' spiritual books and 'New Awakening' home study courses are available through Amazon booksellers and all main bookshops. New Awakening distributes our full range of multimedia home study courses. Visit our website at **www.new-awakening.co.uk**

'Naturally You Publishers' also supply a range of sports psychology interactive home study courses. These 'Into the Zone' mind coaching interactive courses are available for golf, snooker and other popular sports. For details visit our website at **www.into-thezone.co.uk**

Table of Contents

Introduction and Background

New Awakening

Love Healing & Wisdom

Spiritual Courses for your Development and Enlightenment

We are delighted to share with you our 'New-Awakening' courses to bring about your Personal Development and Spiritual Enlightenment. This complete healing experience enables absolute understanding of the mind body and spirit connection. Study all the courses in the five stages to achieve amazing results. Many students have accomplished in one year what would normally take 10 to 20 years of practice to achieve! The secret to this phenomenal growth is in the combination of Divine Reiki healing with an ancient eastern mystical wisdom philosophy as practiced by Dr Usui himself. The courses link together holistically and are expressed in logical, understandable everyday language, offering a total healing experience that will transform your life into a new experience of inner richness and enjoyable connectedness to the world around you. This truly is a revolutionary inner awakening approach, based on the source of creation – Unconditional Love.

The first stage of your development will establish an emotionally secure positive personality centred in love, able to heal and with the ability to create your own chosen destiny. To build this solid foundation three courses have been selected: The 'New Awakening Reiki Healing First Degree' will teach you how to heal yourself, friends, pets and plants through channelling the purity of the Reiki Universal Life Energy. Emotional healing is achieved through 'Love and Relationships' enabling you to discover the real meaning of intimacy and the secret of creating loving, positive relationships centred in Unconditional Love. 'The Excellent You' will establish positive communication with an understanding of how your mind works in conjunction with the Law of Attraction, teaching you whole mind awareness meditation and creating abundance.

The second stage is achieved by helping others overcome their personal suffering through the magic of 'New Awakening Reiki Healing Second Degree' which deepens your Reiki and teaches you how to send healing long distances without having any physical contact. The training includes free energy attunements available from our website, which empower the student to use the Reiki symbols and their mantras. 'New Awakening' Spiritual Reiki will also attune you to the three spiritual bodies, not previously taught on the Reiki 2nd degree course; you will have a direct spiritual experience of the three energies. The heart goes public and service work becomes part of your life.

In the third stage you will receive the 'New Awakening Reiki Master Degree Attunement'. In studying Dr Usui's personal spiritual practice contained in 'The Gateway to Enlightenment' you will learn how to transform your own personal mind's conditioning and belief systems into the true workings of the universal mind; how to establish 'Divine Wisdom'.

When you practice this system of healing as a tool for personal and spiritual development you will discover first hand that you are supported and guided by a kind and loving universe that will enable you to face all of the modern day challenges that you experience in your daily life.

"I would like to take this opportunity to send you my heartfelt appreciation and encouragement for the great courage that you have shown in embracing and expanding your life. I wish you every success in every area of your life from the bottom of my heart." Robert Bourne – Author and New Awakening Course Creator.

'New Awakening' - About the Spiritual System

Enlightenment throughout the ages is always the same, when a human being awakens to the inner realm of the mystic law of creation. These great personal experiences have been translated into many religious, spiritual and mystical practices that have been taught over many centuries to help society. We have tremendous respect and appreciation for all past different teaching methods because they have brought us spiritually to where we are today.

This is a very exciting time as there is the emergence of a new energy consciousness occurring throughout the world. What is happening is that many of these teachings are now transforming into a direct spiritual experience. There are many individuals who are now awakening to an inner Divine wisdom resulting in a tremendous love and compassion for themselves, humanity and the natural environment. You could say that the seeds of the old spiritual teachings are now transforming; they are now starting to flower within society.

We understand this as a shift in consciousness that is starting to take place on the earth today; the start of a new golden, human-spiritual era for all of mankind to experience. There have been many prophesies which support that this change in consciousness will be happening at this time. The main shift that is taking place in society today is the change in the way that enlightenment is now being experienced.

Throughout mankind's history we have had the experience of isolated individuals achieving enlightenment, teaching disciples who in turn have left teachings and spiritual practices for us to follow. These teachings and practices have been left to help us understand our relationship with the creative source of existence. What we are seeing happen today is quite the opposite whereby personal enlightenment is now being experienced by many individuals. This phenomenon is now slowly spreading throughout the whole of society as each enlightened individual influences others to do the same.

Having had the privilege of this direct Divine experience, the founder of the 'New Awakening' system, Robert Bourne, being aware of this new phenomenon has been divinely guided to create a modern system of spiritual awakening that is appropriate for today's age. This new system enables the individual to have a direct experience of the laws of creation; eventually resulting in personal enlightenment. When you experience this new system of learning in its entirety a new spiritual awakening becomes possible.

The new awakening system, created for modern day living, consists of a series of personal and spiritual development Awakening Teachings plus the four Reiki stages of learning. The Reiki stages of learning contain the traditional Reiki attunements which I am offering to everyone free of charge as my gift to mankind, learning concepts plus additional wisdom practices at each stage of development. These additional teachings provide spiritual experiences that become personal foundations, building blocks for the individual's next stage of spiritual evolution. All the four stages of Reiki interlink into one complete 'New Awakening' personal enlightenment system for the student.

The 'New Awakening' system fundamentally differs from the traditional workshop as it offers the student a direct inner spiritual experience of the teaching that they are learning. As you study this spiritual guide you will receive a 'Spiritual Awakening Transfer', guided from Unconditional Love. This will awaken a direct inner experience and realization for you.

The Unconditional Love energy transfers are contained within these teachings and are provided without charge on my videos. They will attune your chakra system to bring about your spiritual realization of the teaching you are learning; a new awakening with a change in consciousness occurs as a result.

These 'New Awakening' Courses and Workshops will create a successful individual with a compassionate heart. You will have the ability to create your own reality, free from the conditioning and limitations of the self. They will awaken you to your own healing; to your own inner state of Unconditional Love and most importantly to your inner teacher providing you with Divine Wisdom in each moment of your existence. You will learn the workings of human spiritual life within all aspects of your relationships and your personal experience of daily life.

A New Awakening spiritual teacher becomes an automatic experience. This is not based upon attendance of a training course but is based upon the ability to channel Unconditional Love from the crown chakra. 'New Awakening' spiritual teachers will have to evolve to a state of 'Being' that resonates with Unconditional Love, not just attend a training course and collect a certificate, otherwise they will be unable to transfer Divine Wisdom and awaken the spiritual teachings within those they wish to help.

The 'New Awakening Spiritual System' consists of

Five Stages of Development with Seven Spiritual Openings

The 'New Awakening' system has been designed and created from Divine spiritual guidance. The New Awakening system understands that if the student has not opened themselves spiritually at the foundation awakening energy stages of their development, they will be unable to progress to the next awakening stage. This is true even if they have previously undertaken the assumed required training. The truth is that you are one with the Divine, although you may be blocked off from this direct connection with the illusionary beliefs you hold within your soul and mind body. This system gently guides you to unlock this beautiful birthright connection to enable your life to flourish into the amazing person you really are. It is for this reason I have released the secret formula to unlock this mystical Divine connection directly for you. Through following the attunement initiation that I will give you free of charge, you will discover how to reconnect yourself to that which is hidden within you. Yes you do it to yourself; I am just your guide. Beware of anyone who tells you that this is not possible; the very idea is charged with illusion, power and control.

Through releasing the secret to the attunement process I have gone against the need to have another perform the ceremony for you. I have broken the tradition which has been passed down over many years. The reason for doing this is two fold. Over several years the awareness that I have been enlightened to has guided me to release this method of self spiritual attunement to anyone who wishes to experience it. The other reason is that the time is right now for as many people as possible to awaken into their spiritual body. For many lifetimes I have taught these teachings in the traditional way; now is the culmination of my soul's mission to share this directly with you in a new direct way.

All the teachings and stages of development that make up this system have been proven by many students who have verified the tremendous depth of beauty and simplicity of the whole process. You are now in a privileged position to enjoy what others have taken many years to experience by having a direct sharing of the Master's secrets.

There is one fact that I would like to share with you which is in respect to the level of effectiveness a spiritual attunement will have upon you. Anyone who offers you any form of teaching or spiritual experience can only help you arrive at the same level of consciousness that they themselves have obtained. Choose your teacher with great care. Over the last few years I have been involved in the world of Reiki. I have been surprised as to how watered down the teachings have become. This is not a criticism of the teachers of Reiki but as a result of my direct experience. I have met many teachers who did not have any spiritual understanding as to what they are trying to transmit, even teachers who had no faith in Reiki at all! The angelic realm of the Divine will always come forward to make a connection with anyone who desires their presence, so even the students of these teachers will have received great benefit.

The problem with the distortion that has been introduced into this system is a result of the illusions held within the mind of some modern Reiki Masters who, as a result have watered down, complicated and distorted the beauty of this natural healing comforter. It is for this reason that I have released directly to mankind the truth, as far as I have experienced it. I promise you that all of my students have grown in consciousness and those who have been re-attuned by me from other disciplines have experienced a much deeper meaningful spiritual energy experience as a result.

The other concern is that people who try and connect directly with the source of Unconditional Love through by-passing the spiritual foundation training, can awaken their repressed, negative pain body of illusion within their soul. When this happens they can fall into fear, withdrawing from their spiritual self, finding they are unable to cope with their new experience. This dark night of the soul experience can be avoided! The only solution for this person is to go back and work through the stages of spiritual energy opening again. We have discovered that many training courses are purely theoretical and the teachings have never been transformed into personal spiritual experiences; the energy then stays within the mind of the student.

When a spiritual foundation and pathway has been established in the energy system and soul of the student the next doorway can then open; this awakening automatically happens with the 'New Awakening' training. All life experiences will then be met at the soul level with healing, transforming into love and balance.

This also explains why people get stuck on their spiritual journey. For example even though someone may have received the Reiki Masters Attunement or a Oneness attunement, if a foundation stage is by-passed, or the chakra energy system has not fully opened, the student will not be able to fully awaken to the next stage of development. This is controlled by the natural law of life. In this example the enlightenment of the Reiki Master's heart chakra will not fully open and be personally experienced if the three energy bodies have not been awakened at the Reiki second degree stage of spiritual awakening. Enlightenment just 'IS' - you are unable to buy it - you have to awaken to it.

The 'New Awakening' method has a compassionate methodical approach through providing proven energy experiences which build upon each other creating a solid safe foundation for the student. This compassionate system created for the individual will enable the next spiritual opening to naturally occur safely. 'New Awakening' will support you with Divine Wisdom, Healing and Unconditional Love.

The 'New Awakening' system also provides three wisdom based companion personal and spiritual home study courses, with tutorial CDs, to support the seven spiritual openings. These courses are contained within the book and seven CD set 'The Seekers Guide for a New Awakening' and the courses are 'The Excellent You, 'Love and Relationships' and 'The Gateway to Enlightenment'.

When the CDs are listened to repeatedly, they have a transformative effect upon the consciousness of the listener. The 'Ah Ha' moments just keep coming over and over again. What could not be understood through reading alone becomes an enlightenment experience as the change in consciousness occurs at the soul level of awareness within you.

When you clear the blocks, transform your illusions, you naturally awaken to your own Divinity. Great spiritual teachers who have spontaneously awakened to their true nature, like Eckhart Tolle, try to encourage us that this natural Divine state of being is really here 'In The Now' and that we are just veiled or blocked off from it by the illusions within our own mind. The students who have studied all three 'New Awakening' courses contained within 'The Seekers Guide for a New Awakening' have accelerated their spiritual development. Enlightenment 'IS' 'here and now', it is our illusions and misguided beliefs held in our karmic soul body that prevent us from having it all – right now! The courses will provide you with a wisdom foundation at your soul level to prepare you to have this birthright experience of Enlightenment.

To achieve the beautiful experience of personal enlightenment we have discovered that the following foundation spiritual gates, when opened within you in the following order, provide a gentle soul transition for this beautiful experience to naturally occur:

First Spiritual Opening: The free attunement to Reiki Universal Life Healing Energy as experienced in Reiki First Degree. This opens the heart chakra and the individual begins their spiritual journey; they are on the pathway to direct enlightenment. It is advisable to study the Reiki courses manual and follow the exercises contained on the tutorial CDs. The home study of the three 'New Awakening' companion courses contained in 'The Seekers Guide' is now introduced to you to assist your spiritual learning experience.

Second and Third Spiritual Openings: This is the attunement and awakening to the energy of the present, the power symbol for physical healing with its complementary emotional symbol of Love. The second and third spiritual openings are experienced within part one of the Reiki Second Degree course manual together with the free Reiki Second Degree spiritual self-attunements. These two symbols form the base two parts of a triangle and when opened allow the soul to soul connection to occur in a more powerful way through the crown chakra as described in stage three. The base chakra is grounded with the power symbol as it brings Divinity into 'the present', the material expression of daily life. The heart chakra, the cross-roads of the lower and higher self, is directly connected to Unconditional Love through the emotional symbol, providing greater love and compassion to be experienced.

Fourth Spiritual Opening: The attunement to the distant healing symbol. This happens through the crown chakra directly through the Divine chakra. 'The divinity in me meets the divinity in you'. This enables the Divine spiritual healing experience directly from soul to soul to occur. This explains the awareness of white light with the out of body experience reported by many of our students. This fourth spiritual opening is experienced within the Reiki Second Degree course manual and through following the guidance contained on the tutorial CDs.

Fifth and Sixth Spiritual Openings: The attunement to Reiki Master's energy. When the spiritual openings one to four have been established the heart chakra of the student can now fully open, radiating Unconditional Love for all of mankind. It is at this stage that 'New Awakening' differs from most Reiki methods used in the West as it includes an additional attunement to Divine Wisdom. This awakens the higher self within the third eye chakra of the student. This connection accesses the Divine Laws of creation enabling life choices to be made with Divine Wisdom, as opposed to personal intuition. This transforms illusion into enlightenment.

Seventh Spiritual Opening: This self attunement completes the journey of the soul by ascending to the crown chakra. The heart chakra compassionately radiates the Reiki Master Energy, the soul transcends to the crown with the higher self moving down from the crown to reside in the third eye. Healing and Wisdom now combine, being expressed as the Unconditional Love of the Source of creation. This is the stage of mysticism, of becoming. Life becomes the experience of bliss, wisdom and oneness with all existence. The individual moves beyond religious, race, national prejudice, written teachings or dogma. It is at this stage that the 'New Awakening' spiritual teacher is born.

Traditional Courses Versus New Awakening Courses

The Universal Life Healing Energy has been traditionally taught in three stages known as the Reiki First Degree, Reiki Second Degree and Reiki Master/Teacher. The students are usually required to take their own notes, or are provided with a basic course manual, at the workshop. Traditionally, Reiki has been taught in the West orally. This means that the student has to remember what the teacher is saying which can cause some stress. This system can create the possibility of the 'Chinese Whispers' syndrome whereby information changes or becomes distorted.

In contrast, the New Awakening system has addressed this problem by providing the student with fully comprehensive multimedia learning material thereby negating the necessity to take notes. This enables the New Awakening student to fully enter into the energy experiences contained within the manuals and through following the tutorial guides experienced on the interactive CDs. The attunements are provided free of charge and you can repeat them as often as you like.

New Awakening teaches The Universal Life Healing Energy in three stages; Reiki 1st Degree, Reiki 2nd Degree, Reiki Master/Reiki Master Teacher, with each stage consisting of two parts. The first part is the professional home study multimedia course learning material. The second part is the practical 'Self Attunement' energy experience, that is provided free of charge as our gift to you from our website. (www.new-awakening.co.uk)

The Story of Sharon

"After a good few years of enduring the usual life struggles, including ill health and relationship issues, my partner treated me to a much needed long weekend away at a health spa. This was where I had my first Reiki treatment. It was the most amazing experience of my life to date alongside child birth. I came away from the weekend knowing that I would be spending at least the next 6 months trying to work out what had actually happened to me.

In September 2007 I began my search on the internet reading various descriptions of Reiki, when I came across the New Awakening website. Robert described his study of many different forms of Reiki and had not limited himself to one style, as had other teachers. Having an engineering background, this appealed to me, as I am always looking for logic, reason and proof in what I learn.

Realising the need to understand the experiences of my first Reiki treatment, I plucked up the courage to call Robert. Shortly thereafter I received the first Reiki degree course hand book through the post. I remember being told at that time, that if I did not want to experience change, then this was not the course for me. Sat here a few years later, I cannot believe how poignant those words now seem.

I spent the next few months reading through the course material in snippets of spare time, fitted between my young family, an engineering design job, running a house and maintaining a long distance relationship.

It was December 2007 when I met Robert and joined a couple of other students on the Reiki I course.

Reading through the material at home I had felt very comfortable with understanding the technicalities of a basic Reiki treatment. However, being on the course and actually feeling and experiencing the energies was quite something else. I felt I was now truly on the path to discovering what I had experienced in my first Reiki treatment.

Receiving my first attunement was like becoming aware of a whole new dimension to life which had been previously hidden from me. I remember feeling an amazing sense of inner peace but also being surrounded by bright and vivid colours.

The opportunity to give my first Reiki treatment in a caring and supportive environment gave me the courage to realise that this was something I could actually do. With a new radiant glow on my face and my 1st Reiki certificate in hand, I set off to increase my experience of this wonderful new dimension. I spent the next six weeks practicing my new found skills on myself, friends and family. The positive feedback I had from other people was amazing and I became a very popular person. At the same time I was also noticing many personal changes which were highlighted to me by using the 21 day journal.

As time progressed my confidence grew and with so many people around me now interested in Reiki, I decided to continue my studies and sent away for the Reiki II course. I also studied the additional courses 'The Excellent You' and 'Love and Relationships', both of which I still refer to today.

During the home study period of Reiki II, I found many questions answered. From the practical aspect of Reiki I had many experiences where I felt guided to certain positions without knowing why. All these experiences I now find were being described in this course. I was also conscious of the fact that in the past I had always struggled with the process of learning and with retention of information. However, I now realised a new ability and enthusiasm to learn. This spread into other areas of my life too.

At the beginning of March 2008, I attended the Reiki II course. Before arriving for this course I already felt very comfortable with giving Reiki treatments and with understanding the course material. I came away feeling I had reached a whole new level on my personal journey. I was amazed at the effect of experiencing the energies using alternative methods such as chanting and humming. During my second degree attunement, the colours visible to me became brighter. I came away feeling a great sense that there was a much longer journey ahead of me than I had first anticipated.

I went home and continued giving Reiki treatments and found that the basic principles of Reiki had now reached into every part of my life. I could see my own failings more clearly and began working on becoming a better person with a life of value and quality.

From the Second course I also returned with the 'Gateway to Enlightenment' manual. I spent the next six months reading and studying this book. This was a much more challenging text and included some new scientific ideologies for me, which I found very interesting. The proof of distance healing behind me placed me in a much better position to grasp these new realities. 'The Gateway to Enlightenment' currently lives by my bedside and a year on I can still pick it up and gain 'Ah Ha' moments.

To continue my journey, towards the end of 2008 I gave Robert a call to discuss continuing on to Masters Level. After a lengthy conversation and some time for me to think things through I concurrently booked the Masters and Master Teacher courses. Receiving the relevant manuals with only just a month to go before the practical I was not sure if I was going to be ready, but reading through the manuals made me realise that I had learnt a great deal from the Gateway to Enlightenment and I was definitely ready for this now. I was really looking forward to this course with no hesitation or doubt, a real change in character for me.

In January 2009, I was given the gift of the Masters attunement, which personally became my biggest and best step.

Through studying the Gateway to Enlightenment and the other accompanying courses, I gained many understandings with my mind which had a significant impact on my life as a whole as I became more understanding of people, emotions and reactions. I then began to find that life does not surprise you in a way that it did before. You start to see things much earlier giving you time to be better prepared, as opposed to living in a constant reactive style.

My Masters attunement really did bring all the teachings to life in a way that I could not have understood before. During the attunement itself, I was aware of many different faces joining my being; an experience for which I have no words.

The following morning I had the amazing experience of waking and finding I not only clearly remembered the dream I had that night, but I also understood it immediately with a deep sense of knowing. I then had the realisation that my mind had understood and learnt from the teachings but before the attunement my heart and soul had not understood these lessons and I felt a shift of the level of understanding to my subconscious.

Now I feel a connection not just between body and mind which comes from Reiki I and II, but also now the connection with the soul. The best way for describing this feeling is to imagine that it is a cold winter's night and you have had a good meal and you are wrapped up warm and comfortable in front of an open fire and are surrounded by all the people that are closest to you. This is the feeling which I now carry with me all the time and it is the most beautiful experience.

After the Masters followed the Master Teacher course which felt like a very natural progression.

I am now looking forward to teaching this beautiful system of healing for the self and others and will continue with Reiki healing for those that do not wish or are not yet ready to make the journey. I shall continue my personal study and self healing and look forward to an interesting and challenging future.

Life carries on but I am now able to deal with issues that arise with more speed and confidence. Having heightened intuition and plenty of new life skills enables you to recognise signs of approaching tests in your life. This whole process becomes apparent as you look back on your life. Occasionally I am able to see where it is going. However you're never quite sure how things are going to happen, so life remains full of surprises.

I would like to take this opportunity to offer my sincere thanks to Robert for his continuing support and his dedication to spread the understanding of Reiki and Spirituality to the Whole World".

Namaste   Sharon Tucker

Home Study Plan of Action

How to Study this Multimedia Course Material

Preparation

1. Read this manual all the way through quickly to get the idea of what you are going to learn
2. Watch the Healing Treatments Video
3. Listen to Healing Tutorial CD (Optional)
4. Prepare your 21 day journal – Start day one of your journal when you receive your attunement to Reiki healing; when you use the Attunement Video.

Practice – (Remember to record everything in your journal)

1. Before you use the Attunement VIDEO complete 'The exercise to feel the energy between your hands' see page 60-61.
2. Attune yourself to Reiki Healing using the VIDEO provided – see page 22.
3. Repeat 'the exercise to feel the energy between your hands' again. Notice the difference the Reiki Energy Attunement has made to your energy field! (If you are unable to notice any difference use the Attunement VIDEO again this time with greater feeling, letting go of the mind as much as possible, just following the instructions).
4. Once you can switch on your Reiki practice the Western Self Healing for three days as shown on pages 64-67.
5. After mastering the Western Self Treatment method - Practice the Japanese Self Healing Visualisation on pages 68-70.
6. Now try the Reiki Well Being exercise on pages 88-89. Try using your hands plus your mind to send the Reiki Healing and notice what happens.
7. You can now practice your healing on a friend either on a couch as shown on pages 78-84, or on a chair as shown on pages 85-87.

My gift to you, a spiritual resource for the world

I have provided FREE OF CHARGE part two of your course which is the Attunement. I have also supplied FREE OF CHARGE three tutorial Videos which show you how to give Reiki Healing treatments on a couch, on a chair and how to scan the aura. Please go to our website at **www.new-awakening.co.uk** to view these videos as often as you like.

There are no restrictions as to how many times you can view these videos.

How to use the Reiki 1st Degree Distant Attunement Video

1. Watch the VIDEO all the way through on your own, in a place where you won't be interrupted, to get the gist of what is going to happen. Unplug the phone etc.

2. To feel a deeper experience continue by relaxing your state of mind by doing the Breathing Meditation listed at the back of this manual. This will prepare you to attune yourself more effectively.

3. Then replay the Video again from the beginning, this time taking 3 deep breaths, this centres your awareness in your sacral chakra, moving your energy down from your mind. Relax and close your eyes. Now imagine that it is you sitting in the chair receiving the attunement.

4. When instructions are given, this is when I will now be talking to you and guiding you through the attunement. Following the sequence - you can either do the instructed actions physically or see yourself doing them in your imagination.

What is Reiki Healing?

It is the magic ingredient which will bring your course to life!

This is the attunement which is on the free Video

The contents contained within this Manual are factual information, new concepts and ways of thinking that are extremely important for your learning. You will learn through studying the theories and concepts. Many perhaps will be new to you and there may be some ideas that you are familiar with; whatever the case it does not matter.

To study this manual may we suggest reading it all the way through quickly to gain the general understanding of its contents and then re-read it slowly over a period of time, one that suits your learning speed. After you have done this we would then recommend that you pick up the manual when you are in the mood and open it at a place to suit yourself and just read that section. By doing this repeatedly, even if you are aware of the contents, the conscious mind will reprogram your previously held beliefs about how life works transforming your understanding at a level of unconscious awareness.

You naturally change without making any effort

It is through conscious mind repetition together with total mind-body relaxation, when you produce a change in your energy state, then the contents will become a part of you, revealing their positive qualities for you beneficially, naturally, in your everyday life. They become a conditioned reaction to your interactions with other people without having to make conscious effort. The most important thing is to become whole as a person. This manual is only half of the solution; the attunement to spiritual universal life energy completes the course and makes it come alive. This is fantastic for you because without even trying your unconscious mind will automatically produce a balanced lifestyle for your happiness.

Just by reading this manual you will change in a positive beautiful way. However the most important aspect that most people totally misunderstand is that the attunement you will receive is the key to unlocking your total experience on an energy and information level.

Changing and attuning your consciousness to an energy that contains more wisdom, more love and healing then you are already connected to is the aspect that really changes your life for the better. The interesting thing is that you are already connected to this source of energy but you are blocked from it; so in reality what is going to happen to you is an unblocking - a reconnecting to something that you already are. It is like removing the clouds that are hiding the sun so you can feel the warmth of the sunshine once again.

What is the Spiritual Attunement?

The energy attunement opens a channel for the universal life energy to flow through to wherever it is most needed on a physical, emotional, mental and spiritual level. The Reiki Master also understands that he or she is only a channel. In a Reiki healing session for example, the practitioner does not direct his or her own personal energy to the recipient but merely serves as a conduit for the universal life energy. The attunements help to cleanse and clear any obstacles that might be blocking your capacity to receive and transmit the energy - a capacity that is natural to all of us.

The effectiveness of your attunement will depend upon the quality of the inner connection that your Reiki Master has achieved on an energy level. I have been very fortunate to have had an enlightened fusion experience in the mid nineties. It was through this experience that I realised my mission was to be of service to others by helping them re-connect to this same wonderful universal source of inner connection, to help empower the individual, creating a balance between their emotions and their mind; a whole person happy and at ease with their life.

All the Reiki courses use the traditional Usui Reiki attunement initiation method as taught in the West. The Reiki healing energy is balancing and therefore healing.

The attunement will bring the material in this manual to life

The attunement will open aspects of you that were previously hidden and closed off from your awareness. You will discover a higher mind existing within you; you will experience a sharpened intuition which will affect all your perceptions and consequently the choices that you make. You will experience a new inner strength and confidence but most importantly you will feel supported, becoming independent, acquiring the time to love and share with others in a new and more meaningful way. This book together with listening to the sound of my voice on the CD sets creates inner transformation; this will enable an inner shift of consciousness to occur within you. Please enjoy your transformation, I congratulate you.

Keeping a 21 Day Journal

Welcome to the wonderful world of spiritual transformation. The first part of this course is to receive your attunement to the Reiki healing energy, your gift from the Beloved Divine Universal Consciousness - indulge yourself, bathe in its beauty.

Firstly get into the habit of performing your daily self healing session. By calling up this gift you allow yourself over a period of time to be set free from all limitations and illusions, to experience the Bliss and Wisdom of Enlightenment.

Nothing can happen if you do not take action! What is this action? It is simply to work on yourself; no one else can do this for you. The Divine cannot do this for you, it does not come from the outside; it comes from the purity of your own desire within your own heart.

I will share with you everything I have learnt and experienced to help enable you to achieve absolute happiness. Please believe me when I say that you are a very important and treasured person. You now have many Divine beings waiting to love and help you on your very special unique journey. You have a very important part to play in this spiritual transformation as you now have a new partnership, one between you and the Beloved Divine Universal Consciousness.

Think of this new relationship in terms of Eternity, as a Love affair that will never end. We all have many illusions and misguided beliefs that are working in our lives at a level below conscious awareness. The very first change in thinking that you need to embrace is as follows:

When you change spiritually on the inside the outside changes naturally, effortlessly and without the use of will power.

This means that the secret to your life changing, which will include all of your relationships, is in the understanding that your spiritual body has been vibrating at a certain frequency; it has a predominant life condition, a certain consciousness and it is at this level of vibration that you have been experiencing your life. It is as if you have been wearing a pair of coloured spectacles that have tainted your vision and have limited your experience. How do you remove the glasses to see clearly?

When you change your inner life frequency to a higher Divine energy level your life will vibrate outwards throughout the universe at this new vibration. To change on the inner spiritual level will bring new and better situations to you. This will bring positive change to all that you are connected to. Over time, painful experiences, all of your relationships will be transformed into beauty and value and you will simply experience that any negative connections you have had will start falling away from you.

To keep a journal is really important because it will show you the subtle changes that are happening to you as you begin to grow in awareness as your spirituality develops. This journal will lay the foundation for your change when you go on to take the next development course of Reiki 2nd Degree. Many people are waiting for some big miracle to happen and want only to record that event, however the Divine is very gentle and pure and it is the subtle changes that happen daily that over a period of time will make a tremendous difference to who you will become in the future. I promise you that you will not regret starting this very special spiritual journal.

Dr. MIKAO USUI   THE FOUNDER OF MODERN REIKI

The Reiki story begins in the mid 1800's with a teacher, Dr. Mikao Usui, searching for the ancient healing system used by Christ, Buddha and all the ancient great healers. His quest enabled his final accomplishment of achieving enlightenment. It was through his inner realizations that he gained the wisdom to help others and developed the Reiki system of healing.

Dr. Usui started by opening a school to teach his spiritual teachings, he also offered individual healing sessions for physical illness and emotional distress.

What is Reiki?

The word Reiki means 'Universal Energy'. Eastern medicine has always recognized and worked with this energy, which flows through all living beings and is vital to the well-being of life. The energy is known as 'ki' in Japan and 'chi' in China and 'prana' in India. Acupuncture, tai-chi and yoga are also based on the free-flow of this energy in a person.

As a therapy and a personal development tool, Reiki is an effective and simple way of tapping into this energy and activating it for the benefit of the receiver, to stimulate the body's own natural healing potential. Reiki is a complementary non- intrusive method of helping heal a variety of illnesses; physical, emotional and mental.

What can Reiki do for you?

In Reiki, the quality and flow of your own inner healing energy is what determines your physical and emotional health and well being. When you are unwell you are experiencing a block in this natural universal healing energy and that blockage shows itself to you as illness or emotional distress and pain. Most people when receiving Reiki healing report they experience relaxation, a sensation of warmth or coolness and some see colours in their inner third eye.

The Reiki healer acts as a channel for this healing energy like switching on a light switch in a dark room reconnecting you once again, allowing the flow of your own inner healing energy to bring your body, mind and emotions back into balance and harmony, restoring you back into a state of well-being and health.

You are a Channel for Reiki Healing

The ability to channel Reiki to give yourself and others healing comes after you have received a special energy attunement. The energy attunement opens a channel for the universal life energy to flow through to wherever it is most needed on a physical, emotional, mental and spiritual level. The attunements are normally given by a Reiki Master-teacher. New Awakening has released this secret and shows you how you can attune yourself. The students have the opportunity to progress in their learning through three Reiki degrees, each one deepening and strengthening their capacity to serve as a channel for the universal life energy.

In a Reiki session, the practitioner does not direct his or her own personal energy to the recipient but merely serves as a conduit for the universal life energy. The Reiki attunements help to cleanse and clear any obstacles that might be blocking your capacity to receive and transmit the energy. This is why it is recommended to repeat the Attunement regularly.

Traditional Reiki Healing Courses

Reiki has been traditionally taught in three stages known as the Reiki First Degree, Reiki Second Degree and Reiki Master/Teacher. The students are usually required to take their own notes, or are provided with a basic course manual, at the workshop. Traditionally, Reiki has been taught in the West orally. This means that the student has to remember what the teacher is saying which can cause some stress. This system can create the possibility of the 'Chinese Whispers' syndrome whereby information changes or becomes distorted.

In contrast, the New Awakening system has addressed this problem by providing the student with fully comprehensive multimedia learning material and distant attunement videos, thereby negating the necessity to take notes. This enables the New Awakening student to fully enter into the energy experiences.

New Awakening Reiki Healing Courses

New Awakening teaches The Universal Life Healing Energy in three stages; Reiki 1st Degree, Reiki 2nd Degree, Reiki Master/Reiki Master Teacher, with each stage consisting of two parts:

1. Professional home study multimedia course learning material
2. Practical 'Self Attunement' energy experience, that is provided free of charge as our gift to you from our website. (www.new-awakening.co.uk)

The Connection Reiki has with our Body and Energy System

Reiki works with the endocrine system and regulates hormone balance in the body and metabolism. On an energetic level, the endocrine glands correspond to and interrelate with the chakras in the energy body. This powerful natural energy is available to all of us and sustains our lives every day. It is this energy that we draw on in the course of our daily activities. In a utopia our lives would be perfectly in balance as they would be naturally supported through interactions with others in a loving environment. We would have appropriate rest and relaxation, fresh air, clean water and wholesome, natural food. Of course, our lives and environments are not in perfect balance. This is where the power of Reiki Healing can help everyone.

The Principles of Reiki are an introduction to your spiritual development

Just for today I will live with the attitude of Gratitude

Just for today I will not worry

Just for today I will not anger

Just for today I will do my work honestly

Just for today I will show loving kindness and my deepest respect for every living thing

What is Reiki Lineage?

A lineage can be compared to your family tree. In the case of spiritual teachings and especially in the Buddhist tradition a teaching is passed from the Master to the disciple and then passed on unaltered to preserve and contain the original intention and teaching of the Master. The purity of lineage is dependant upon the teaching not changing as it is taught from one Master to the next.

"The reason I have experienced and received many different attunements from different Reiki Masters was to establish, as best I could, the purity of original teaching as taught by Dr Usui. Below you will see two of the five different Reiki lineage trees that I am connected to. This enables me to pass to you the very best representation of Dr Usui's teaching that is possible. I very quickly discovered that the tradition of orally transmitting the teaching without documentation was the preferred method up until recently. This very traditional method of teaching is about 3000 years old. The teachings shared in the west originate mainly from Hawayo Takata when she became a Reiki Master in 1938. It is now established that the teachings had been altered in their transmission from Dr Usui to Dr Hayashi who introduced a medical and Christian approach to healing losing some of the spiritual methods used by Dr Usui. I am pleased to know that Dr Usui's original intention and teachings are now re-emerging providing us with Reiki teachings reflecting the master's original intention."

In this example Robert has two Reiki lineages that go directly back to the source of Western Reiki and Reiki from Tibetan Buddhism. He trained with one of the few Masters initiated by Hawayo Takata, who introduced traditional Usui Reiki to the Western World.

Traditional Usui Method	**Tibetan Reiki Method**
Dr Mikao Usui	Dr Mikao Usui
Dr Chujiro Hayashi	Dr Chujiro Hayashi
Hawayo Takata	Hawayo Takata
McFadyen	P L Furumoto
Himani	William L Rand
Tanmaya Honervogt	Hazel Raven
Robert Bourne	Padma O'Gara
	Fran Hardiman
	Robert Bourne

Reiki History

Where does Reiki come from?

Reiki was developed by a man called Mikao Usui. Usui grew up at a time when Japanese society and culture was going through a period of rapid change. It was not until the 1850s that Japan opened itself up to the Western world; for two centuries starting in 1641, all Europeans except the Dutch had been expelled from Japan. The Chinese and Dutch that remained were confined in special trading centres in Nagasaki and no Japanese were allowed to leave the country. Christianity was declared illegal and all Japanese were forced to register at Shinto temples. Those Japanese who refused to renounce Christianity were executed and so were a few Christian missionaries who refused to leave the country. This ban on Christianity was not lifted until 1873. It was the United States that finally forced Japan to open its borders and open its economy to the outside world and this event led to a great flood of new ideas and esoteric systems coming into Japan from all over the world.

Not only that, but Japan underwent a period of rapid industrialization, transforming itself from a feudal society into an industrialized nation - able to compete with the West on an equal footing - within a period of only 30-40 years. Such a period of rapid change created a real climate of wanting to keep hold of traditional culture. Japan was looking for a spiritual direction and people wanted to rekindle and maintain ancient traditions, while embracing the new. This is what Usui did when he developed Reiki. In the time when Usui was growing up, Japan was a melting pot of new ideas, with many new spiritual systems and healing techniques being developed. Reiki was one of these systems.

Mikao Usui's Life

Mikao Usui was born on August 15, 1865 in the village of 'Taniai-mura' (now called Miyama-cho) in the Yamagata district of Gifu Ken (Gifu Prefecture)and he died on March 9, 1926 in Fukuyama. He had an interesting life. He grew up in a Tendai Buddhist family and had a sister and two brothers, one of whom studied medicine. As a child he entered a Tendai Buddhist monastery near Mt. Kurama ('Horse Saddle Mountain'). He would have studied 'kiko' (the Japanese version of Chi Kung) to an advanced level - and maybe practiced projection healings - and he was exposed to martial arts too.

From the age of 12 he trained in a martial art called Yagyu Ryu - Samurai swordsmanship - in which he attained the level of Menkyo Kaiden in his 20s, this being the highest license of proficiency in weaponry and grappling. He continued training in the Arts and reached high levels in several of the other most ancient Japanese methods. He was renowned for his expertise and highly respected by other well-known martial artists of his time.

In his younger life he experienced much adversity, lack of money, no security or regular employment. It is not known why; it could have been due to bad luck or simply that he did not attach importance to material things. He was regarded as something of an eccentric. He married and his wife's name was Sadako. They had a son (born 1907) and a daughter. Usui followed a number of professions: public servant, office worker, industrialist, reporter, politician's secretary, missionary and supervisor of convicts. Usui was private secretary to Shimpei Goto, who was Secretary of the Railroad, Postmaster General and Secretary of the Interior and State. The phrase 'politician's secretary' can be taken as a euphemism for 'bodyguard'! It is during his time in diplomatic service that he may have had the opportunity to travel to other countries. In 1868 (when Usui was 3) there was restoration of rule by Emperor, the Meiji Restoration. Mutsuhito reigned until 1912 and selected a new reign title - Meiji, which means enlightened rule - to mark a new beginning in Japanese history. It is known that Usui travelled to China, America and Europe several times to learn and study Western ways and this practice was encouraged in the Meiji era. At some point Usui became for a while a Tendai Buddhist Monk, or Priest, (maybe what we in the west call a lay priest) but still having his own home, not living in the temple. This is called a 'Zaike' in Japanese: a priest possessing a home.

Usui Sensei was interested in a great many things and seems to have studied voraciously. His memorial states that he was a talented hard working student. He liked to read and his knowledge of medicine, psychology, fortune telling and theology of religions around the world, including the Kyoten (Buddhist Bible) was vast. There was a large University library in Kyoto and Japanese sources believe that he would have done most of his research there, where sacred texts from all over the world would have been held. He studied traditional

Chinese medicine and Western medicine, numerology and astrology and psychic and clairvoyant development.

Usui also took Zen Buddhist training in 1922 for about three years. Many different spiritualist/healing groups were in existence at the time and one of these - attended by Usui - was 'Rei Jyutsu Kai'. Today this organization consists of the most spiritual monks and nuns in Japan, psychics and clairvoyants.

The Roots of Reiki

The system was rooted in Tendai Buddhism and Shintoism. Tendai Buddhism (a form of mystical Buddhism) provided spiritual teachings and Shintoism contributed methods of controlling and working with the energies. Usui had a strong background in both kiko (energy cultivation) and a martial art with a strong Zen flavour (Yagyu Shinkage Ryu) and he also took Zen training and these studies may have contributed in some way to the system that he developed. There also seems to be a strong connection between Usui's system and Shugendo (mountain asceticism). Shugendo was a blend of pre-Buddhist folk traditions of Sangaku Shinko and Shinto, Tantric Buddhism, Chinese Yin-Yang magic and Taoism.

Usui's Associates

Morihei Ueshiba　　　　**Onisaburo Deguchi**　　　　**Mokichi Okada**

During his life, Usui associated with many men and women of very high spiritual values. Some were famous people in Japan, for example Morihei Ueshiba (founder of Aikido), Onasiburo Deguchi (founder of Omoto religion) and Toshihiro Eguchi (founded his own religion and was a good friend of Usui). There are even connections between Usui and Mokichi Okada, the founder of Johreiand Jigoro Kano, the founder of Judo.

Usui the Man

Usui Sensei could be very outspoken, apparently and controversial. His friends would often be concerned about his welfare. His answer to them would be 'just for today do not worry', one of the Reiki precepts. According to one of his surviving students, Usui was physically big; quiet in manner and extremely powerful. He did not suffer fools gladly and could be quite abrasive at times. He could become righteously angry and quite impatient, particularly with people who wanted results but were not prepared to work for them.

Usui's Motivation

But what prompted Usui to pursue all these studies? Well, according to Hiroshi Doi, a member of the Usui Reiki Ryoho Gakkai in Japan (see later), Mikao Usui was wondering what the ultimate purpose of life was and set out to try to understand this. After some time he finally experienced an enlightenment: the ultimate life purpose was 'Anshin Rytsu Mei' - the state of your mind being totally in peace, knowing what to do with your life, being bothered by nothing. Doi says that with this revelation, Usui researched harder, for 3 years, trying to achieve this goal. Finally, he turned to a Zen master for advice on how to attain this life purpose. The master replied "If you want to know; die!" Usui-sensei lost hope at this and thought, "My life is over". He then went to Mt. Kurama and decided to fast until he died.

So it seems that, according to Hiroshi Doi, Usui was looking for a way of knowing one's life's purpose and to be content and despite all his exhaustive research, he could not find a way to achieve this state. The monk's advice prompted him to go to Mount Kurama and to carry out a 21-day meditation and fast. We now know that Usui Sensei carried out a meditation called 'The Lotus Repentance', which comes from Tendai Buddhism. Usui carried out the meditation and, according to his memorial stone, he experienced an enlightenment or 'satori' that led to the development of Reiki. But this does not seem to have the ring of truth to it, because he performed the meditation five times during his lifetime and Usui's system wasn't something new that came to him in a flash of inspiration, but a system that was rooted in many existing traditions. Usui was already teaching his system long before he carried out the meditation. Originally, Usui's system did not have a name, though he referred to it as a 'Method to Achieve Personal Perfection'. His students seem to have referred to the system as

'Usui Do' or 'Usui Teate' (Usui hand-application). The name 'Reiki' came later, perhaps first used by the founders of the 'Gakkai.

Mount Kurama where Usui carried out one of his meditations is a holy mountain. It is near Kyoto, the former capital of Japan, a place which I heard described on a recent television travel programme as being 'the spiritual heart of Japan' - a place with a thousand temples representing a whole range of deities. Mount Kurama is also important from a martial arts perspective, being the place where mountain spirits - Tengu - are said to have given the secrets of fighting to the Samurai. Morihei Usheiba, founder of Aikido, often took students to the mystical Shojobo Valley to train.

Usui Sensei Teaches his System

According to Usui's memorial stone, Usui was a very well-known and popular healer and he taught nearly 2,000 students all over Japan, but this should be taken as just meaning a large number, maybe 1,000 or more though. All of his students started out being treated by him. Usui would give them empowerments so that they were connected to Reiki permanently, so they could treat themselves in-between appointments with him and if they wanted to take things further then they could begin an open-ended program of training in his system. His teachings were very popular amongst the older generation, who saw them as a return to older spiritual practices; Usui was teaching at a time of great change for the Japanese people. In April 1922 Mikao Usui opened his first 'Seat of Learning' in Harajuku, Tokyo and he used a small manual which had come into use about 1920. It did not contain any hand positions for healing others: it contained the Precepts, Meditations and the Waka poetry.

Of the people whom he taught, 50-70 went on to the first level of Second Degree and maybe 30 went on to the second level of Second Degree. Usui trained 17 people to Shinpiden level. There were 5 Buddhist nuns, 3 Naval Officers and nine other men, including Eguchi who was said to have been Usui's main friend/student. Eguchi later formed his own religion called Tenohira-Ryouchi-Kenyuka, which was Shinto revivalism, getting back to the early Shamanic roots. Even to this day in Japan there is a spiritual community which carries on Eguchi's tradition, where they carry out a simple hands-on treatment technique based on the use of intuition and involving simple initiations. Usui's teachings were what is called a 'Ronin' (leaderless) method. This was to make sure that no one person could lay claim to them and they would be freely available for all who wanted to learn them. It would have been more usual for Usui to have kept his system as a Usui family method, rather than passing it on to outsiders.

Usui Sensei did not only practice and teach his Spiritual Teachings in his school but he also gave healing. He became very well known for his healing skills and his fame spread very quickly throughout Japan. In 1923 the Kanto earthquake struck 50 miles from Tokyo, destroying Tokyo and Yokohama. An estimated 140,000 people died from the 'quake or the fires that followed it. This was the greatest natural disaster in Japanese history and Usui gave many treatments to victims. The Usui Memorial says that Usui Sensei "reached out his hands of love to suffering people" and in recognition of his services to the people during this emergency he was awarded an honorary Doctorate. It is when he was giving healings at a Naval base that he met a group of Imperial Officers, who became students, including the man who would be responsible for allowing Reiki to come to the West.

Mikao Usui died from a stroke in a town called Fukuyama in Hiroshima in 1926.

Some Unusual Students

The Imperial Naval Officers were Jusaburo Gyuda/Ushida, Ichi Taketomi and Chujiro Hayashi. It was certainly surprising to Usui's students that Usui would teach such people as Officers of the Imperial Navy. Indeed, it seems that there was some 'resistance' to this taking place and Usui's friends were upset that he would teach his spiritual system to military men. But Usui had been doing some healing at a naval base and it seems that there was some metaphorical 'arm twisting' that led to the officers learning Usui's method. But Dr Hayashi, certainly, does not seem to have been interested in the 'spiritual path' aspects of Usui's system, he was a Christian and he focused on the treatment aspects, which was not really so important from Usui's point of view. Usui modified his teachings accordingly, to meet the needs of his new students. Since Dr Hayashi - and probably the other Naval Officers too - were having difficulties in experiencing the energies, Usui and his senior student Eguchi introduced something new into his system: the symbols that are so familiar to Western Reiki practitioners.

Dr Chujiro Hayashi

Chujiro Hayashi was born in 1878. He graduated from Naval School in 1902 and by the time he was doing his Master training with Usui Sensei in 1925 he was 47 years old, a former Captain in the Imperial Navy and he was a Naval Doctor. He and the other Naval Officers Ushida and Taketomi were the last people to be taught by Usui. It seems that Hayashi was one of Usui's less experienced Master students since he may have trained with Usui for only 9 months. When you reached Master level with Usui, this represented the commencement of a long period of training which culminated in learning the connection rituals and considering that other students of Usui spent 9 months meditating on only one energy at second-degree level, Dr Hayashi cannot have learned the inner teachings of Reiki in such a short space of time, nor reached the higher levels of Mastership. Together with the other naval officers, Dr Hayashi was a founder member of the Usui Reiki Ryoho Gakkai, a 'memorial society' set up after Usui's death. The 'Gakkai was described by Tatsumi (one of Hayashi's Master students), rather disparagingly, as an 'officer's club'.

Although he was one of the founding members of the 'Gakkai, he left, it seems, because the nationalism displayed by the other officers conflicted with his Christian beliefs and went against Usui's teachings and because of the many changes that the other Imperial Officers were introducing into the system, for example the introduction of many kiko (Japanese QiGong) techniques. But Hayashi changed things too, as we'll discover shortly.

After he completed his training, Hayashi opened a clinic with eight beds and 16 healers working there and clients were treated by two or more people. He kept detailed records of the treatments that were given and used this information to create 'standard' hand positions for different ailments which ended up being published in the training manual given to the Gakkai's students (the Usui Reiki Hikkei). In fact this work had already been started when Usui was alive and it seems that Dr Hayashi was carrying out the research with Usui's knowledge and approval. Usui was interested to see if his spiritual system would 'stand alone' as a healing system. This guide to 'hand positions for different ailments' is very much trying to mould Reiki into the 'medical model', where you diagnose a particular ailment and then prescribe a particular set of hand positions to deal with it, very different from Usui's simple and intuitive approach.

Despite this research though, Hayashi still expected his students to be able to use advanced scanning or intuitive techniques to work out their hand positions, with his 'standard' positions as a fallback position.

Dr Hayashi founded his own society in 1931, five years after Usui died. It was called Hayashi Reiki Kenyu-kai, which means Hayashi Reiki Research Centre. Since Dr Hayashi had made some changes to the system he had been taught by Usui, he was honour bound to change the name of the system, but the changes that he introduced were not popular: some of his senior students left the school, including Tatsumi, who believed that the teachings were no longer Usui's. Hayashi's focus was very much on hands-on healing. Dr Hayashi would teach First Degree over a five-day structured course, with each day's training taking 90 minutes and students would receive his more complicated attunements on four occasions during this training, by way of echoing Usui's weekly empowerment sessions. Dr Hayashi trained 17 Reiki Masters and produced a 40 page manual which contained the hand positions for different ailments. Since Dr Hayashi would not have been taught Reiju by Usui Sensei, it would appear that he learned the technique when Eguchi joined the Gakkai for a year. Eguchi seems to have joined out of respect for Usui, but he was put off by the nationalism of the Gakkai members and left. Presumably there was enough time for Hayashi to have learned the connection ritual and this ritual seems to have been modified by him. Certainly the ritual that was taught to Tatsumi is not Usui's Reiju and neither is the ritual being used by Mrs. Yamaguchi, another of Dr Hayashi's Master students.

Chujiro Hayashi died on May 10th 1940. Sadly, he took his own life; it seems that he was very concerned at the build up of nationalism in his country and it was the threat of war that led to his death. Dr Hayashi's wife Chie continued as President of his school, teaching in the 1940s, but their children did not continue the clinic.

Hawayo Takata

Hawayo Takata was born in 1900 on the island of Kauai, Hawaii. She came to Dr Hayashi's clinic suffering from a number of serious medical conditions that were resolved through Reiki, but she was originally intending to receive conventional Western medical treatments for her tumour, gallstones and appendicitis. The story goes, though, that on the operating table (just before the surgery was about to start) Mrs Takata heard a voice that said "The operation is not necessary". She is said to have refused the operation and asked her Doctor if he knew of any other way to restore her health. The doctor referred her to Dr. Hayashi and she began receiving a course of treatments.

Mrs Takata was quite sceptical about Reiki. She felt so much heat from the practitioners' hands that she was sure they were using some sort of electrical equipment - maybe little electric heaters secreted in the palms of their hands! She looked in the large sleeves of their Japanese kimonos, under the treatment table, but of course there was nothing there. Her scepticism turned into belief as her health problems resolved themselves and she decided that she wanted to learn Reiki for herself.

Dr Hayashi wanted to teach Reiki to another woman besides his wife (someone who would not have to be called up to fight in a war) and since Mrs. Takata was so persistent he decided to teach her to Master level, which happened in 1938. Dr Hayashi gave Mrs Takata permission to teach Reiki in the West and she did so in the USA. She was the 13th and probably the last Reiki Master that Dr. Hayashi initiated and between 1970 and her death in 1980 Mrs Takata taught 22 Reiki Masters. Until quite recently, all Reiki practitioners in the Western world derived their Reiki from this lady and could trace their lineage through her to Dr Hayashi and Mikao Usui.

The original twenty-two teachers have passed on the Reiki tradition and Reiki has spread throughout North and South America, Europe, New Zealand and Australia to many parts of the world.

It is almost impossible to estimate the number of Reiki Masters and practitioners in the world, but it must run into tens of thousands and millions, respectively.

But it cannot have been easy for Mrs Takata, teaching a Japanese healing technique in the United States, after the Second World War, with memories of Pearl Harbour still in everyone's minds. The American population was not particularly well disposed towards anything connected with Japan. Also, while nowadays people are continually exposed to magazine articles about feng shui, tai chi, traditional Chinese medicine, meridians and alternative medicine in general, at that time in the United States these ideas must have seemed to have come from another planet. Mrs Takata was trying to transmit her whole culture and a totally alien one as far as her students were concerned.

For this reason, Hawayo Takata was forced to modify, simplify and change the Reiki that she had been taught by Chujiro Hayashi, in order for it to be acceptable to the Westerners that she dealt with and the Reiki that she had been taught by Dr Hayashi had already been modified by him after he had been taught by Mikao Usui. Not only did Mrs Takata have to modify the practices of Reiki, but she also felt obliged to put together a story about the history of Reiki to make it more acceptable to a hostile American public. Out went Mikao Usui, Tendai Buddhist and in came Dr Mikao Usui, Christian theologian, who travelled the world on a great quest to discover a healing system that explained the healing miracles that Jesus performed. So stories about Usui being a Christian Doctor, going on a world-wide quest and studying theology at various universities along they way, are not true. Despite this, they are repeated in Reiki books, even ones that have been published recently.

As well as putting together a Reiki 'history', Mrs Takata ended up being referred to as 'Grand Master' of Reiki, to make a distinction between herself and the Masters that she taught. This is an office, position or title that was not envisioned by Mikao Usui. Reiki is not based on the idea of gurus or great masters to whom one has to pay homage. Unfortunately, some people in the Reiki community are greatly wedded to the idea of 'The Office of Grand Master' and what I see as the narrow and dogmatic view of Reiki that is approved by the current incumbent, Mrs Takata's grand-daughter, Phyllis Lei Furumoto.

Reiki in Japan

Now the story turns full circle and Western style Reiki has returned to its country of birth. At one stage people believed that Reiki had died out in Japan and that the only Reiki that remained in the world was the Western version. But Reiki Masters who moved to Japan in the 1990s discovered that there were Reiki practitioners there who were doing things that were very different from the Reiki that we had become used to in the West. It was also discovered that there was an association called the Usui Reiki Ryoho Gakkai (Usui's Reiki Healing System Association) which to begin with seemed to have been established by Usui. Now we know that this is not the case. The Gakkai was set up as a sort of 'memorial' society by the three Naval Officers. Tatsumi described it as an 'officer's club' and now it has almost the sort of place in Japanese society that Freemasons occupy in the West: most people have heard of the 'Gakkai, but they are not quite sure what they do. You need to be a member if you are going to get on in business or in politics.

As well as the 'Gakkai', there are other Reiki practitioners in Japan who use Reiki to varying degrees following Usui's original form of Reiki.

Now Japan is experiencing a big explosion of Reiki, but it is mostly Western-style Reiki. Over time I am sure that the two forms of Reiki will join and blend, combining the basic traditions of Usui Reiki with the creative experimentation that characterizes the Western approach to the system.

(New Awakening honours and has great respect for Dr Usui. Having left no stone un-turned in our spiritual system we have re-introduced the Tendai Buddhist spiritual practice embraced by Dr Usui. Reiki healing is perfect in itself but traditionally in the west it has been taught in isolation and not as a fundamental part of a spiritual wisdom philosophy as em-braced and practiced by Dr Usui himself. The New Awakening spiritual system embraces both aspects, unconditional love and wisdom. Reiki healing comes from the aspect of uncon-ditional love. The New Awakening system provides you every tool that you will require for your personal transformation of consciousness and spiritual enlightenment. We highly recommend at this stage of your study that you obtain a copy of our book "The Seekers Guide for a New Awakening" which contains the wisdom element).

We would like to say thank you to Taggart King for his sincere research as shown above on establish-ing a true picture on the history and origin of Dr Usui Reiki healing.

An Everyday Reiki Help Guide

The Uses of Reiki Healing

Health

Pain - In most illnesses people experience pain. Giving a Reiki treatment can significantly reduce or relieve pain in many conditions. By applying Reiki healing to the site of pain directly, immediate relief can be felt.

Hospital patients - When visiting relatives or friends in hospital have you ever felt helpless and purely in the hands of the medical profession to provide comfort to them? It is wonderful to feel empowered that you can now do something to accelerate their recovery. Give them a Reiki healing treatment even if only by holding their hands as this will be beneficial.

The important point to remember here is that Reiki will travel through their energy system throughout their whole body therefore helping to accelerate the recovery of the cells and bring a natural healing energy boost to their immune system.

To quote an example, a friend who had recently been involved in a car accident astounded the doctors by the rapid healing of her broken bones and tissues. Several people had been giving her Reiki healing since the injury and she was able to have her stitches removed and leave the hospital many days earlier than expected.

Terminal Illness – This delicate subject is one of the most emotionally distressing situations a person can experience. To watch a loved one deteriorating with, for example, cancer and not be able to do anything can make one feel so helpless.

We have had the privilege of witnessing many miracles where complete remission has occurred as a result of daily Reiki healing sessions. You are now in a position to actually take some action to alleviate their suffering and your suffering.

With respect to this subject the NHS has endorsed and employed Reiki healers for this very purpose. The reluctance of the NHS to administer expensive drugs in the case of what they consider terminal illness is becoming more commonplace today leaving the family members angry and frustrated. Reiki healing now empowers you to do something for your loved one.

Accidents and injuries - How often has a member of your family sustained a minor injury at home, work or school or whilst playing sports? Reiki healing will, at a cellular level, definitely accelerate tissue repair bringing about speedy healing to the injury.

With injuries it is best to apply the Reiki healing directly to the damaged area if possible. If it is not possible to touch the damaged area hold your hands about 3 inches (about 7cm) above the injury. Reiki will travel through space, blankets and clothes! To help with the emotional shock of the injury you can place your hands on the solar plexus (above the navel on the higher stomach area). Also on the adrenals which are above the kidneys around waist level on the back of the body.

Boosting the Immune System – Wellness is dependent on the strength of a person's immune system. Reiki healing will definitely boost the immune system enabling the body to heal more quickly and fend off bacteria, viruses, common ailments etc. helping to promote an improved level of vitality and stamina.

Emotional Upsets

Learn to relax and release stress - Stress and anxiety are a major cause of ill health today and over a period of time can build up and be the cause of depression, nervous conditions and inability to relax and to relate in a happy way. When your partner comes home in a stressed state a Reiki healing session will help to calm them rapidly and enable them to enjoy their leisure time more fully.

Any general Reiki healing treatment would be helpful, particularly the Reiki Exercise for Enhancing Wellbeing on page 88 to 89 or if time any of the full Reiki treatments as described either on a chair or on a couch.

Sleep well at night – If you or your family have difficulty in sleeping a Reiki healing treatment whilst in bed just before going to sleep will be really helpful.

We have noticed that when treating others, working on the feet and the lower part of the body is very effective, therefore treat the lower three chakras, 1, 2 and 3 on page 51 and healing treatment positions on page 83. This has the effect of bringing the energy down from the mind into the body changing the breathing pattern to that of relaxation and tranquillity.

When working on yourself, when you come to sending the energy to your feet, guide it with your imagination as taught in the Japanese Visualisation method of self healing on pages 68 to 70.

Arguments – Such a common problem within families. Wouldn't it be lovely if every couple could heal each other?

To calm down the emotions and take the heat out of the situation, first start by Reiki-ing yourself. Place one hand on your solar plexus and one hand on your heart chakra and allow the Reiki to flow until you feel calm and at ease with yourself.

You are now in a position to offer Reiki to your partner or your child or whoever is upset. Use the same hand positions as used on yourself above and wherever you feel intuitively guided to put your hands.

Loss of a Loved One – As a Reiki healer you can offer comfort to any family member or friend who is experiencing the pain of loss. Our experience shows that to receive Reiki in these circumstances provides tremendous emotional support and a feeling of being loved and comforted.

Shock and Trauma – In today's modern society and with the reality that life is constantly changing outside of your control most of the time, it is no wonder that shock can come upon us at any time without warning. Reiki will be your comforter without doubt.

Please keep your Reiki flowing until you feel centred and able to accept whatever has happened. Therefore as with all emotional pain start your Reiki healing on your heart and solar plexus chakras, followed by whatever you feel drawn to do. Remember you can't do it wrong as Reiki will flow to wherever it needs to go.

Children

Minor ailments – Cuts and bruises, scrapes and scratches, childhood ailments such as measles and chicken pox, upset tummy, ear ache etc. can all be helped with Reiki healing. How much better you can feel if you can help your child directly with healing energy which they respond to so beautifully.

Help your children with learning and their exams - We have found that Reiki will help with concentration and will prepare the mind to learn in a holistic way using the whole mind, which will assist with long term memory. This is obviously beneficial with learning facts and information.

For exams a Reiki healing session before the exam is useful to help remove nerves and stress, preparing the mind and the person to achieve the best they can. It is also worth mentioning to give yourself a Reiki healing session so you are sending calm feelings to the person you are supporting and not feelings of anxiety which could unsettle them. This section applies to adults as well as to children.

The Elderly

Getting older – Arthritis, degeneration of organs, loss of memory, pain and discomfort, mobility problems, more frequent admission to hospital and operations are all more common as we get older. Reiki is so effective in helping all these problems and can be used as described previously. You will find that an easing of symptoms occurs and wounds heal more quickly. General mobility can be greatly improved and the person will feel cared for and loved by you. It will also help to develop a better relationship as a result. This could be viewed as a time to give something back to those who have helped you in your early years.

Happiness

Creating happiness – When you give yourself or others a Reiki healing treatment you will notice that over a period of time your emotional feelings will begin to become calmer and you will be more comfortable and at ease with yourself, thereby gaining a sense of inner contentment.

What is very beautiful is that you will gradually become happy on the inside without the dependence of waiting for external events to occur that bring about a temporary form of rapturous happiness. With Reiki healing you will gain an inner tranquil happiness; an inner peace.

Beauty

Rejuvenation – With constant Reiki treatments you will start looking and feeling years younger with increased vitality. You will shine with radiance and inner beauty giving you a glowing complexion. Many women have reported the reduction of facial lines and wrinkles. A little tip - if you use Reiki healing with your imagination, which means to visualise yourself the way you would like to look, the rejuvenation process will accelerate.

Animals

Your pets – It's likely that those of you who have pets already experience a deep, loving bond with them. Reiki can vastly deepen that bond and you will also know the joy in helping to heal and support them.

When your pet is receiving veterinary treatment, Reiki will assist and speed their recovery. It will also help them in their old age in the same way as it helps elderly people.

When you are giving your animal a Reiki healing treatment don't worry if they just get up and go as they will know when they have had enough for that session. Once they have experienced Reiki they will also tend to come and ask for Reiki healing when they want it.

Plants and your food

Indoor and outdoor plants – When arranging a bunch of flowers place your hands over the flowers and switch your Reiki on. Send your Reiki to the flowers and watch them smile! Seriously, you will discover that cut flowers last longer when given a Reiki treatment as it improves the vital energy force within them.

Before planting seeds in the garden, hold them in your hand and give them Reiki healing energy. As a general boost to your garden plants go around your garden on a regular basis giving them Reiki energy. You will be rewarded with a wonderful healthy looking plant display.

(On the Reiki Second Degree course you will learn how to send Reiki to the whole garden at the same time in one session).

Your Food – Reiki your food before cooking and eating. It really does increase the life force energy within your meal and it harmonises your food with your body. You can Reiki water before drinking and Reiki wine; in fact you can Reiki everything you eat and drink.

Honouring plants – Please take a moment to honour the plant world as it supports our lives in many ways. For example plants give us air to breathe as they are a major source of oxygen. They also breathe in the carbon dioxide we exhale and purify many of the countless pollutants in the air.

Plants give us the food we eat – without them we would starve. Plants are also a major source of beauty that definitely enriches our lives.

Reiki is your gift to yourself. Use your Healing Hands effortlessly, continuously - anywhere, any time, in any situation for example when eating, or travelling on a bus, when at a business meeting – or even when you're sleeping!

A Definition of all Reiki Healing

There are many types of Reiki, each Master adding their own interpretation. Whatever the type of Reiki the definition is the same:

1. The process of Attunement to the Spiritual Universal Healing Energy.
2. A lineage. Starting with the one who first channelled Reiki then listing the family tree of Master Teachers that followed their teaching method.
3. Reiki does not require the mind of the person to guide the energy. Reiki is a Spiritually Guided Life Force Energy, all knowing from a higher unlimited power; it has an intelligence of its own, although it follows your intention.
4. Reiki can do no harm.

How Reiki Supports Physical Health and Emotional Wellbeing

- Reiki heals holistically on all levels; physical, emotional, mind and spirit
- Reiki can be combined with most complementary therapies, such as hypnosis, NLP, Kinesiology, Aromatherapy and Massage.
- Balances the main organs and glands plus their bodily functions
- Eliminates and helps to clear toxins within the body
- Helps and soothes chronic illness
- Releases stress and brings relief to pain
- Treats the symptoms of illnesses

- Changes the consciousness of the causes of illness
- Balances the energies and chakra system in the body
- Strengthens the universal life-force energy within the body
- Strengthens the immune system
- Reduces and relieves stress
- Releases suppressed harmful emotions, trapped negative feelings
- Promotes natural rejuvenation and self-healing
- Will achieve a deeper state of meditation
- Will connect you to your intuition
- Strengthens and deepens your intuition
- Promotes creativity
- Reiki healing will always support the natural healing process

Strengthening your life force

On a physical level, Reiki helps to strengthen and sustain the body's immune system. The body is then able to defend itself against the effects of environmental pollution and contagious diseases. The kidneys, liver and digestive organs are better able to deal with the toxins they encounter and flush them out of the body.

Caution and guidelines for your safety with Reiki

The exercises, hand positions and meditations described in this course manual are intended for the healing and harmonization of you as a holistic being. The course creator wishes to point out that, in the case of illness, a doctor or healing practitioner should always be consulted. The Reiki positions and meditations described may naturally be applied as an additional form of treatment. Reiki does not take the place of conventional medicine. Always consult your doctor for an acute or infectious condition and any problem of urgent concern.

Reiki is a complementary therapy that works effectively alongside orthodox and alternative health-care solutions.

The Seven Chakras

7. Crown Chakra – Violet

6. Brow Chakra (3rd Eye) – Indigo

5. Throat Chakra – Blue

4. Heart Chakra – Green

3. Solar Plexus Chakra – Yellow

2. Sacral Chakra – Orange

1. Root or Base Chakra - Red

Chakra is a Sanskrit word meaning wheel and the chakras can be seen as coloured, circular energy vortices or put simply, coloured discs. Energy exists in three forms: light, sound and vibration. These three forms are basic to the creation of the universe.

The best way to consider what the chakras are is to think of your body as being a Rainbow body of light. If you look at the chakra colours you will see they are the same colours as a rainbow. When we are born the soul enters this world through the first chakra, the red coloured chakra at the base of the body; this is known as the physical birth. After birth we then have the opportunity to evolve in consciousness, to develop from an animal human into a spiritual human; this awakening of the spiritual dimension is known as the second birth. The third and final stage of your evolution is the completion of the soul's journey; the spiritual birth, obtaining Oneness with the cosmos and all of Divine creation. When this happens it is experienced as pure bliss and is the highest form of consciousness that is possible as a human spiritual being.

The spiritual Divine white golden light comes first and splits into seven different energy vibrations creating the rainbow body of light for your soul to enter. These seven chakras or energy centres then create and sustain the physical body enabling us to live our lives. The physical body is known in spiritual terms as the body of action.

Once we are born the spiritual white golden light is accessed through the crown chakra. When you are attuned to Reiki Healing this energy becomes a comforter for our lives because it acts like a bridge between the spiritual human heart chakra of love and the crown chakra of the white, golden light of the Divine. The Divine is a source of higher consciousness which we can access at will because it exists within us, as it created us. Reiki Healing connects us directly to this inner source of creation to provide us and others Healing and Unconditional Love.

In terms of Reiki healing it is important to understand that the spiritual Divine energy came first in our life as it is the source of our existence; it is this unchanging pure aspect that created our life and is accessed in a Reiki healing session. When you understand that this energy came before the body, you will soon realise that if you are having a problem in the body physically, mentally or emotionally the quick solution is to go to the source that created you. In that way you will bring in its healing balancing energy and it will return you back to perfection once again. This is the quick route to the creation of miracles. When you understand this, the only thing you need to do is to change your consciousness to a higher consciousness than your own. The good news is that this exists within you now as it created you! Your job is to let go and allow it to work for you. Reiki Healing will re-connect you to this inner source.

When you carry out a Reiki Healing treatment you will soon see the connection between the hand positions and the locations of the chakras; you will discover that the most effective treatments are those where you send healing to the chakra locations. This understanding will help you to learn the suggested healing hand positions very quickly. When you give a healing treatment just remember where the chakras are located in the body and then place your hands there.

In Reiki it is not normal to give healing to the crown chakra as this is left open for the Divine energy to flow freely. This is why Reiki is known as channelling spiritually guided healing energy. You act as a channel, connect with Reiki and the Divine higher consciousness knows where the healing is required.

As you develop in spiritual awareness you will discover that you are one with this source of creation. The people who develop the quickest are those who can keep an open mind to new possibilities and to new understandings of life's workings. Those with fixed minds will find it harder to grow in consciousness. Keep your mind open having a child like curiosity and innocence about how existence is.

I would like to introduce you to how the chakras affect us. There is a direct relationship between our physical, mental and emotional health and the main energy centres in the body know as the chakras. The chakras relate to the body through the endocrine system and the nervous system. Everything that happens in your life begins or is created in consciousness. This is transferred into existence through the chakras and then into the body, experienced right down to every cell. This is why if you want to change your life you will need to change your consciousness; the way you think.

Reiki healing creates a change in consciousness, this then creates a change in the energy field through the chakras which creates a change in every cell in the body; this is how Reiki Healing works.

The chakras are a part of our consciousness, or spirit and they are the way in which our higher self is connected to our physical and mental selves and the way in which we experience our lives on Earth. The chakras are constantly changing as they receive and transmit energy and information every moment of our lives. Energy and information is constantly changing and in turn so do our chakras; if you could see these constant changes, some people can, we would look like a light show!

Physical, mental or emotional problems cause the chakras to be out of balance. Sometimes just one chakra will contain these imbalances or it could relate to several chakras. Reiki healing is a perfect way to realign the chakras to perfect harmony and balance. Each chakra relates to a different aspect of our life as explained below.

Understanding what each Chakra does

The crown chakra is the only chakra that is outside of duality. It is the connection to your higher self, a state of completeness. Through the unconditional love of Divine higher consciousness all things that have been previously separated come together in oneness. It is the source of your eternal self and the centre of spiritual purpose; your connection to spiritual guidance.

When the sixth chakra opens to the Divine self, the world becomes a meditation of golden tranquil light. You experience each moment from a graceful state of Divine wisdom. The sixth chakra transmits and receives information unconsciously from one person to another. This is known as personal intuition.

The throat chakra is the centre of self expression, communication and speaking your truth. It is also the chakra for healing. This chakra is healthy if we are fully able to express our ever changing selves truthfully. This chakra heals by listening to others totally. It also receives audible spiritual information.

The heart chakra is the centre of unconditional love and compassion. When open to the Divine it is the flowering of the Reiki Master; the expression of the angelic realm with compassion for all humanity, animals and nature. The heart chakra is a crossroads between the higher three chakras and the lower three chakras, blending our base animal human nature with our higher human spiritual nature.

The solar plexus chakra is the seat of our personal power and will, the self or ego. Our passion for life, action and mind concentration are all controlled by this chakra. This is the seat of the logical mind and intellect. Emotional control issues are also felt in this chakra.

The sacral chakra is the light centre of creativity. It is the centre of our sexuality. It is all about human emotions and passion. This chakra is very receptive to the emotions and feelings of others and motivates us to express passion and creativity through music, art, poetry and love making.

The base or root chakra is about the physical aspects of our life. It expresses our connectedness to the earth and our basic need for survival; our home, money, our possessions, to eat, defend ourselves and procreate for the survival of the species.

Understanding the basic relationship between the Chakras

- The top three chakras relate mainly to our human spiritual selves.

- The heart chakra is like a mediator between our physical and spiritual selves.

- The lower three chakras relate mainly to our human physical selves.

- The hand chakras (in the palms of the hands) are used for Reiki healing. These are also connected to the heart chakra and the throat chakra.

- The foot chakras are connected to the base root chakra of our existence and ground us to the earth.

All of the chakras may be expressive and receptive; however the odd numbered chakras tend to be more expressive than receptive. These chakras are more to do with the masculine energy. Men and women each have both masculine and feminine aspects. The masculine energy may be thought of in terms of expressing, giving or a motive force. They go outwards into life and reflect how we express ourselves. The right side of the body is more connected to the masculine energy.

All of the chakras may be expressive and receptive; however the even numbered chakras tend to be more receptive than expressive. These are more to do with the feminine energy. Men and women each have both masculine and feminine energy. The feminine energy may be thought of in terms of receiving and creating. We experience our life inwardly, more emotionally, our inner awareness with inner processing of our life's experiences. The left side of the body is more connected to the feminine energy.

Advanced Techniques Taught on the Reiki 2nd Degree Course

Chakra Balancing: There is a technique called 'Chakra Balancing' that allows you to balance each individual chakra to regain their positive function

Beaming: It is possible to beam Reiki energy to your client from across the room

Distance Healing: This is the ability to send healing without a physical connection to other people, places or situations anywhere in the world.

What are Affirmations?

An affirmation is a self-suggestion to change a negative thought pattern into a positive one. They are self empowering and are created with positive suggestions.

Quantum physics now understands that our thoughts, our consciousness is creating the reality in which we live! The Law of Attraction explains that what we think goes out to the universe acting as a magnet, attracting back to us the very same thing that we thought about.

An affirmation is a positive phrase that is said to yourself or out loud with passionate emotion for the purpose of creating a new experience for your life. When it is said out loud it becomes more powerful because you are using the throat chakra which sends a vibration into the physical realm of existence. You are therefore expressing your intention to the universe.

The more you use a positive affirmation the more effective it will become. The best way to overcome any negative pattern is to use your affirmation when giving yourself Reiki self-healing. Because this is a direct pathway to the Divine core of your being, change will become quickly noticeable.

Use your affirmation for a minimum of 21 days. The more you use it, the stronger the new pattern you wish to achieve will become.

Below are positive affirmations that relate to each chakra. You can use these positive affirmations to assist healing the mind and emotions.

ALL PURPOSE AFFIRMATION

I am a spiritually enlightened child of the Universe, perfectly created to live in balance and harmony with all that is around me. My life is part of the natural plan and my presence on earth is welcome as I am most wanted. I offer myself as a gift to others as I am part of and essential to the oneness of all existence.

SEVENTH CHAKRA AFFIRMATION

I am a spiritually guided enlightened child of the Universe. I serve the highest good of my personal spirit and that of the creative source of all things. I am fully committed to bringing joy, unconditional love, Divine wisdom and healing to the earth.

SIXTH CHAKRA AFFIRMATION

I look for the beauty in all things. I am willing to see the truth with acceptance and love. I see into life for its hidden treasures. I see Divine spirit within all of existence.

FIFTH CHAKRA AFFIRMATION

I speak my truth clearly and without hesitation. I listen with discernment and goodwill for the true communications of others. I am ever open to hearing the voice of my higher-self as I embrace myself as a human spiritual being.

FOURTH CHAKRA AFFIRMATION

My heart is open. I freely give and receive the healing power of unconditional love. I am loved, lovable and loving.

THIRD CHAKRA AFFIRMATION

I am in charge of my life. I decide what is important and meaningful. I set clear boundaries and honour those of others. I surrender my personal will to my higher Divine self.

SECOND CHAKRA AFFIRMATION

I am fully alive. I appreciate and honour all my feelings and fully embrace my creativity and sensual life.

FIRST CHAKRA AFFIRMATION

I am grounded and calm. I am rooted to the earth. I am welcome, wanted and completely supported by the Universe.

Reiki Healing Treatments

Self-Treatments with Reiki

You will soon learn how to heal yourself as well as to treat other people. By treating yourself daily with the Reiki energy you will discover that your connection with the source and your channel for the Reiki healing energy will become stronger. This will establish a clear strong channel for the Reiki energy to flow smoothly and intensely through your energy channels and chakras.

Spiritual masters understand that you are unable to heal others until you have healed yourself; a balance is required with your Reiki treatments. I would say to start with, give yourself seven self-healing treatments to every healing treatment you give to another. The Reiki First Degree is mostly concerned about healing yourself.

When you are giving Reiki treatments you are channelling universal life energy and therefore you also receive a Reiki treatment whenever you treat someone else. However this is not as effective as focusing your intention upon yourself when you give yourself a self-healing treatment. In this way self-treatments can be a useful way to make sure you maintain a strong connection with the Reiki universal life energy everyday.

There are two approaches in doing self treatments; one method is the Western-style that was created by Dr. Hayashi, the other is the original Japanese Usui self treatment. We believe in offering you both approaches so that you can choose for yourself what suits you the best as an individual. Both approaches have immense value.

Getting Started – The first step

I would suggest that you practice the first exercise listed below to become aware of your own energy before using the Attunement Video. First become aware of the energy field around the body known as the Aura. When you have done this attune yourself to Reiki Healing and then do the exercise again, noticing the difference the Reiki energy has made to your energy.

On our website you will find the Distant Attunement Video which will be the second thing you need to do – Attune yourself to Reiki Healing. Please take time to read the instructions on how to prepare the room and yourself before you use this Video. Remember to watch the Video first to get an understanding for what you are going to do. Once you have done this re-play it. This time it will be for real as it is you who is being attuned. Enjoy the experience. Remember to do the breathing exercise, which you will find in the exercises at the back of the book, to prepare yourself before you start the Video for your self-attunement.

Once you have attuned yourself to Reiki Healing, practice the exercise again to feel the energy between your hands. Prove to yourself that your Reiki Healing is flowing and it has made a subtle energy difference.

Exercise to Feel the Energy between your Hands

Healers can learn to read the aura and gain information about the person's state of health and well being. This ability will be helpful to learn as it will show where the aura is weak and requires strengthening through Reiki Healing.

A person's aura will show imbalances, strengths or weakness in their energy field. What does this mean? First of all the aura is an energy field that can be found all around our body. You could say we live inside a field of energy like being inside a cocoon. This energy field can be found any distance outside of the physical body, from one inch to three feet in distance. Many of the Reiki hand positions are directly related to the chakras, which function as openings for energy to flow in and out of physical, mental and emotional bodies of a person; this energy flow is also reflected in the aura.

This exercise helps you to tune into your own energy field which will in turn help you develop energy sensitivity. You will then become more aware of the aura energy field. As you work with this exercise you will notice certain sensations flowing between the fingers and the palms of your hands. Note: Holding your hands, palms facing each other, about six inches apart is a very good way to test that your Reiki Healing is on before you offer healing to another person.

Tuning into your own personal energy field

- Sit on a chair or on a cushion on the floor. Close your eyes and then take three deep breaths, relax your shoulders with each out breath. Allow yourself to let go of any thoughts plus any tensions in your body. Become aware of the in breath going into your abdomen, allowing your stomach to rise and fall with each in breath and out breath. This will help your awareness move down from you head to your heart where your ability to feel and sense energy exists.

- Keep your eyes closed, relax and breathe naturally. Now hold your hands in front of your heart, your chest area. Keep your arms bent at the elbows with your muscles re-laxed, your palms are slightly cupped and facing each other. Your hands should be about ten to twelve inches apart. Hold them in this position for two to five minutes as you imagine the energy building up between the hands. Now very slowly move your hands towards each other. Become aware of the energy field between your hands as they move closer together.

- Very slowly move your hands closer together and then move them further apart, like playing an accordion. Notice what you feel, if you can't feel anything do not worry, you will in time. Some people say that it feels like they have a balloon between their hands. You might get a feeling of tingling and pressure, increased warmth or a tick-ling sensation, like static electricity.

Western Method of Reiki Self Healing

Western-style self-treatments are based on laying your real hands in a serious of hand positions on your head and body allowing the Reiki universal life energy to flow into you. You can see the hand positions for giving yourself and others a Reiki treatment below. Remember that these positions are the ideal and comprehensive method to use when giving a Reiki treatment but they are not set in stone. In practice you will find your own preferred combina-tions based on what you find to be comfortable and based upon where you need to send the Reiki energy. When you are treating yourself or others you can put your hands wherever it seems appropriate.

The traditional Western hand positions are as shown in the illustrations on pages 64-67. A great way to learn this sequence is by following the demonstration on the free tutorial Video. They are the same or similar to those you would learn on a practical training course.

You do not have to always complete a full treatment going through every hand position and treating yourself for 30 minutes. You can do an informal self-treatment using just a few hand positions for whatever period of time you have available. For example if you have just bruised your arm, just treat your arm.

While you are relaxing for a few minutes, maybe watching television, you could have one hand on your heart with the other hand on your solar plexus (the stomach). Discover what is comfortable and is effective for you. While it is better to treat yourself in an undistracted situation because the energy will flow more intensely, any self-treatment is better than no self-treatment at all and can be fitted into the busiest routine if you want it to be.

Most people find it easiest to carry out these Western-style self treatments first thing in the morning upon waking up or last thing at night in bed before falling asleep. If you do not have spare time when you wake up in the morning set your alarm clock half an hour earlier so that you can give yourself a very special start to the day. Many people give themselves a Reiki treatment to enable them to go off to sleep; what better way is there than this?

How to treat 'difficult to reach' areas of your body

Sometimes there are parts of the body that you would like to treat but you cannot get your hands to them because they are awkward to reach - then there are a few choices available for you:

1. You will learn this in the Japanese self healing method. Imagine that your hands are resting on the part of the body that you cannot quite reach and imagine energy flowing into you from the imaginary hands. You are now using your intention to open and direct the flow of Reiki universal healing energy.

2. Rest your hands on your navel or sacral chakra and imagine that Reiki energy builds up in that area and then flows through your body to where it is required.

3. This can be done anywhere and at any time. Imagine that you are drawing energy down through your crown Chakra, the area above the top of your head and then the energy flows through your body directly to the area that requires healing without using your hands.

A few disadvantages of the Western self healing system are: -

1. This self treatment method of placing your hands on different parts of your body is difficult to do in a public place for obvious reasons.

2. Some of the hand positions can feel uncomfortable to hold for any length of time.

3. A lot of people feel very little when doing the hands on self-treatment and can think that nothing is happening.

(The reality is that the Reiki is flowing but you are just not aware of it happening, which can be a little disheartening in the early stages of your practice. Please be assured that this is a common experience, just trust and continue and in time as your sensitivity and channel develops you will realize and experience the Reiki universal life energy as a pure subtle gentle experience. Sometimes I have noticed that it takes about 3 minutes for the Reiki to start flowing. This might be the resistance of the person or the time required to release energy blocks before sensitivity is experienced).

Combining Japanese and Western Approaches

It is possible to combine the Japanese and Western approaches to an extent. The Japanese approach emphasizes to us that you do not have to rest your hands on yourself to do a self-treatment; your intention is enough. If you intend through visualization that Reiki enters your head from a particular point than it does so.

Reiki will follow your thoughts and your intention

To combine the two approaches, sit with your hands resting on your heart and solar plexus and visualize imaginary hands going through the standard five hand positions described in the Japanese method on pages 68-70.

Hand Positions for the Western Reiki Self Healing Method

You can sit in a chair or lie on your back on a treatment couch or reclining chair for this self treatment. You can do this in bed before you get up or before you go to sleep at night. The standard Western hand positions to use for your own self-healing Reiki treatment follow the same body location treatment positions, shown in the diagrams below, as when you are treating another person with a Reiki healing treatment. You can also include your knees at the end of the ten positions shown below, if you are not too relaxed. These positions are only a guide and you can make up your own routine, one that suits you.

Please remember that you are sending Reiki to the main Chakras of the body and because the body system is holistic, which means every part is contained within the whole, if your feet require Reiki the healing energy will flow there at the same time you are holding your hands in another part of your body.

Please keep an open minded, non-limiting attitude when you are self-healing then everything is possible. With Reiki you cannot do it wrong, be gentle on yourself.

1. COVER YOUR EYES - Lay your hands on the right and left of the nose, covering the forehead, eyes and cheeks.

Balances the pituitary and pineal glands. Treats eyes and turns your consciousness to inner self, easing the whole body. This position promotes relaxation

2. TEMPLES: Now place your hands on both sides of the top of your head, above your ears, touching the temples.

This position harmonizes both sides of the brain and has a relaxing and calming effect on the conscious mind. This improves clarity of thoughts, memory and eases depression promoting the enjoyment of life.

3. EARS – Place your hands so that the centres of your palms are over the ears.

This position is good for treating problems with the outer and inner ear. Eases symptoms such as noise or tinnitus, disorders of the throat and nose. Good for colds and flu, worry, depression and hysteria.

4. BACK OF HEAD – Place your hands at the back of your neck at the base of your skull.

This position calms your mind and emotions. This will help release any tension or fear and soothe any headache.

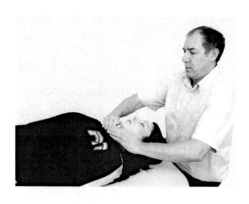

5. THROAT – Hold your hands in V position above the throat, but do not touch it directly.

The throat chakra represents self-expression. When working on this position be very gentle and loving. Can help metabolic disorders, weight problems and low blood pressure.

6. Lay your hands across the upper chest, just above the bra line.

Treats heart, lungs, liver, thymus gland. Increases your capacity for love promoting acceptance and trust because you are sending Reiki energy to the heart chakra.

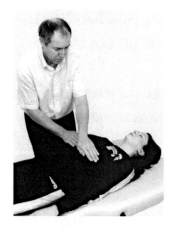

7. Place your hands across lower ribs just below the bra line.

This treats the liver, pancreas, gall bladder, stomach and parts of the intestine. It helps to ease hepatitis, gall stones, digestive and metabolic disorders detoxifying the body.

This position balances the solar plexus chakra.

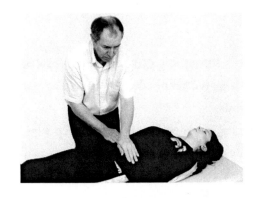

8. Place hands across the navel.

Treats eating disorders, digestive complaints, upper and lower colon and the bladder. Reiki is sent to the sacral chakra which is about lower emotions or passion, creativity, sexuality and personal power.

9. Place your hands behind you on your middle back at kidney height, fingers pointing towards the spine.

This position treats the adrenal glands plus the nervous system. It relaxes fears and shock, enhances confidence. By releasing fear we let go of the past able to live in the present with joy.

10. Place your hands on your groin area with your hands in a V position. Because you are treating yourself it is good to touch this area.

This treats the base chakra which roots us to the physical world. Releases fear and anxiety. It is grounding and centring bringing a sense of personal security.

11. Place your hands on your Knees.

The knees are about releasing anxiety and fear about moving into the future, into the unknown. Helps release pride, stubborn ego and inflexibility. The Reiki will assist you by bringing love, compassion and understanding.

(This position is optional. You can sit up or curl up to reach you knees.)

Japanese Original Usui Reiki Self-Treatment

The original method of giving a self-treatment is something quite new to Western Reiki and only came to the West in about the year 2001. We give acknowledgment to Taggart King in his search for truth in sharing this method with us.

We have provided two ways to achieve this exercise, explained in step 2 and step 3 below. Please try both ways to discover which way works best for you as an individual. It is as if the spiritual you has come out of your body and is directly connected to the source of Reiki Universal Life Energy and is giving the physical you a Reiki healing treatment.

1. Sit comfortably on a chair and close your eyes

2. In your imagination see another you (imagine a copy of you) sitting in front of you with their back towards you. (You will be sending them Reiki healing using your imagination and intention).

3. Alternatively, if you find step 2 difficult to imagine, you could imagine another you standing behind you sending healing to the real you sitting in the chair.

4. In your imagination you are now treating the projected image of yourself by resting your imaginary hands in a series of hand positions on the head. Remember Reiki follows your intention. A Universal Law states 'Whatever you put your attention on energises' and your intention will connect with your higher self to create the required outcome, in this situation Reiki healing.

5. Hold each hand position, as shown in 1 – 5 below, for about 3-5 minutes.

6. While holding each hand position in your imagination focus yourself channelling Reiki through your hands into the imaginary you that is sitting in front of you or the imaginary you that is behind you sending you Reiki. You are acting as the giver and receiver at the same time.

By fixing your intent so strongly, but visualizing and imagining consistently, the energy seems to flow very strongly. If you have a problem with visualization do not be concerned as all this may mean is that you do not use your internal visual sensory system as much as your feeling or internal auditory hearing sensory system. Your visualisation system will develop with practice if you want it to. You can simply intend that the energy is passing into you in these various positions and it will do so without you having to visualize clearly.

As you do this self healing treatment you may feel or get the impression that hands are on your head and body. It is also possible to experience more than two hands in different places of your body at the same time. If you experience this be grateful and enjoy the additional help you are receiving; life is mystical.

Japanese Self Healing Visualisation Sequence

1.   This position is over your third eye

Imagine that your hands are in front of your forehead along the headline, with your hands held with fingertips touching each other over your forehead and your palms are facing towards your face.

2.   This position affects the whole body.

Imagine that your hands are positioned over your temples and are also covering your ears.

3. Calms Mind and Emotions. This will help release any tension and soothe any headache.

Imagine that one hand is cupping the back of your head while the other hand is resting on your forehead.

4. Imagine that both of your hands are at the back of your neck at the base of your skull.

5.   Imagine that both of your hands are resting on the crown of your head and that Reiki universal life energy is flowing down from the crown to your base chakra and then flowing up gently through each chakra back to the brow.

This position will fill you with Reiki healing energy, joy, vitality and you will feel completely refreshed as a result.

The Head is the Focus of your Attention for this Japanese Method

Advantages of the Self-Treatment Visualisation Method

One of the big advantages of this Japanese self treatment method is that it is something that you can do unobtrusively when sitting with your eyes closed anywhere: at work, whilst travelling etc. provided you are not driving.

If you do not have thirty minutes to spare for a Reiki self-treatment, do not worry; just reduce the time given to each of the five imaginary hand positions. It is a good idea though to complete all five imaginary hand positions.

What is exciting about this technique is that it demonstrates that Reiki simply follows your thoughts; it will follow the focus of your attention. You simply use a visualization to focus your intent in a particular way and Reiki does what you intend!

Giving Reiki Treatments to Others

General : Once you have been attuned to Reiki, you only have to place your hands on someone and the energy will flow automatically. It is important that in the first few weeks after the attunement you give as much Reiki as possible, both to yourself and to others. This helps the energy to flow smoothly through the recently opened energy centres, the chakras within your spiritual body. This will establish a strong channel with the source of Reiki universal life energy. The Reiki flows automatically to the areas of need. You could say it has its own intelligence of natural balance and knows where to go to a large extent.

If you try to force the process by willing the recipient to get better your ego starts to get in the way and there may be a general lessening of the Reiki energy available. You need to connect with the source of Reiki universal life energy in a neutral, relaxed and detached way. The more you can relax your mind, your ego, the stronger the Reiki energy flow will become available to you or your recipient.

Remember that you are a channel for the energy and that you are not the source of the healing. This fact explains why treatments do not drain you at all, but actively replenish and invigorate you. It is not your energy that you are dealing with.

Learn to trust in your connection with Reiki: Just trust that Reiki will do the work then allow it go where it needs to. Learn to let go, relax and do nothing except enjoy the experience. How beautiful it is to be supported and loved through letting go in trust and your only action required is to connect with the Reiki universal life energy.

The full Reiki Treatment: A full Reiki treatment will normally last between forty-five minutes to an hour. Start with the shoulders for about five minutes to balance your energy with your client/recipient and then spend about three to five minutes in each of the hand positions. If you can feel a lot of energy passing through your hands in a particular position then you can hold that position for longer, if you feel it necessary. You will usually find after a while the intensity of the sensation in your hands would decrease when the area has taken as much Reiki as it can for that session.

The best results are obtained when you are calm and relaxed, being one with the energy. If you are giving a treatment while having an animated conversation with someone you will not produce the best results because the energy will not flow so strongly. This is why calming relaxing music is a good idea.

Working with your Intuition: When you have had some regular practice treating other people, Reiki may begin to guide you intuitively to place your hands in certain areas of the body that require healing that are out of sequence with the standard hand positions. I think the simple measurement of this becomes apparent in the Reiki flow of energy as it would increase, get stronger when your hands are in a position of need for the receiver. Please don't get caught up with trying to interpret whether this or that should or should not be happening or that you are not doing it correctly.

In my experience there are many intuitive healers who actually misinterpret the situation that is happening and to take this a step further, if you think about it, it does not matter. The reason why it is not important is because we are in a state of constant change moment to moment and the only important quality is to bring love and balance and harmony to the physical emotional and spiritual present moment experience. The Reiki does this by itself so do yourself a favour and allow its energy to love and bring healing to the current situation.

The Reiki energy orchestrates an infinity of events that are beyond our mind's understanding and possible comprehension. This is why a simple approach based on trust is the most powerful opportunity for the greatest effect to occur. It is only the mind that needs to be clever, fearful of losing control, having the tendency to not allow the new to enter as it purports to know everything; in reality of course it is very limited.

Therefore by dropping and relaxing your mind's ego you allow the Reiki universal energy consciousness which is a greater awareness than your own individual energy to bring healing to the situation. You are just starting to learn Reiki and if you can take this principle on board at the beginning of your Reiki training you will produce far greater results than you could ever have dreamed about. The impossible may just now become possible – miracles are made from this understanding.

I would recommend that you use your intuition in the following way. If you have in your mind an impression that your hands ought to be in a particular position then don't think about it, do not analyze it; just do it!

Do not become attached to results of treatments: It is important that you do not become too attached to results and trust that your client is receiving what they need. Remember that you cannot mess up the Reiki treatment; you cannot leave a person worse off than they were to begin with and you are not responsible for the results.

The Reiki First Degree works very simply; when we touch, the energy flows and produces a healing effect and when we take our hands away the energy stops flowing into the person. Hands on equals Reiki on - Hands off equals Reiki off.

Approach treatments with a neutral state of mind not trying to force it or enforce your preferred solution onto the situation. Simply let the energy flow, trust that it is going to the right place.

Create a relaxed atmosphere for your Reiki treatment: Treatments should usually be conducted in a relaxing area where both practitioner and recipient feel comfortable with minimal outside noise and distractions. Make sure that the room is warm, turn the lights down and have some relaxing music playing. You could light a candle and burn some incense.

If the client wishes to talk with the practitioner the treatment will still work. However it is best if conversation is kept to a minimum because Reiki will flow better if you and your client are calm and not distracted by the conscious mind's energy. The reason for this is simple. When a person is thinking and talking it is very difficult to achieve the alpha state of mind, which is required to receive the maximum healing effect. So I would recommend that you ask your client to close their eyes, relax, take a few deep breaths and for this time now just to let go and enjoy the experience; the special time for them. You will discover that usually the Reiki energy relaxes the client so well that this ceases to be an issue after the treatment has begun.

Given the spiritual nature of the healing it is possible for some practitioners to access intuitive information about the client when they are giving the treatment. This happens because the client has relaxed their normal protective conscious mind's energy barrier. You are in a privileged position of great trust and my advice is to respect the privacy of your client and not to mention any of your perceptions. The Reiki energy will heal without the need to discuss any of your client's private personal life's information. If after the healing session the client talks and releases any issue of need for their well-being and healing, this is a different situation because it is client led. If you consider that you have a need to share your intuitive awareness with your client you may need to look at your own issue of personal power and heal your solar plexus third chakra!

Love does not sit in judgement - it is pure acceptance and Reiki is an expression of unconditional love in compassionate action; to bring balance, harmony and healing to every living being exactly as they are. Reiki always works for the greater good in all situations therefore you need say nothing because your client will do all of the work. If they need to talk they will talk. You have to learn to trust - that is all.

Practical aspects of treating someone: Reiki treatments are generally carried out with the client lying down on a treatment couch. This method is probably the most satisfactory for practitioner and client; the client can relax totally and drift in and out of consciousness, without falling out of a chair for example and the practitioner can get themselves comfortable either standing or in the seated position.

If you do not have a treatment table then you can improvise by using a bed or a settee but it is not likely to be very comfortable for you. If you do not have a treatment table it is probably best to use a chair. You could try treating someone on a reclining garden chair with yourself seated on a stool. Whilst you are still practising at the Reiki First Degree level it is not as important as you are not charging a fee for your Reiki treatments. Please make sure you are comfortable when you give Reiki.

A professional couch is a consideration if you want to progress to the Reiki Second Degree practitioner level. When you do this, if you choose, you can then charge a fee for your services. You can of course treat people in the sitting position with the client sitting on a dining chair and this is the way that most conventional spiritual healers do their work. When you do this you can stand in order to reach the head positions and could kneel on a cushion to reach the torso and the legs. It is still comfortable for the recipient but they will not be able to relax as much as if they were lying on a treatment table. It is really important to pay the same amount of importance to your own comfort as well as your client's. In all things balance is required between yourself and others equally, no self-sacrificing please.

Treating the front and back of a client: Most treatments will only be carried out on the front of a person with them lying on their back. I personally do not believe you need to turn a client over to 'do their backs' routinely. In this situation you will have to use your wisdom and decide what works best for you and your client. Turning a client over half way through a treatment can be disruptive to the client as they have to bring themselves back to full awareness to turn over during the treatment. It is best for the client to go deeper into their inner state because the Reiki universal life energy is then being received more effectively; which after all is the intention of the healing session. Remember Reiki will go naturally to where it is required.

Short Reiki Treatments: Although we usually talk in terms of carrying out a full treatment for people over a course of four to six treatment sessions you can give people short treatments by just putting your hands where it is hurting them. For example an athlete with a sports injury can benefit just by you putting your hands directly on the affected part of the injury if you only have a short period of time to provide a treatment. The energy will not have an opportunity to deal with the client's entire energy system that heals on all of the levels but it should deal with the immediate problem and that maybe is all that is wanted.

Detailed Instructions for Giving a Reiki Healing Session

Tune yourself in: Tune yourself into your client's energy. Imagine the closeness between yourself and the person that you are about to treat. Feel your energy field and that of your client beginning to merge. Become one with the recipient; a good way to do this is by starting the treatment with your hands on your client's shoulders.

Dedicate the treatment to the highest good of the client: Dedicate the treatment to the highest good or the highest healing good of your client or to the highest good of all concerned. By doing this you are focusing your intention to open and reveal the Reiki universal life energy to flow into the client to restore balance, health and harmony within their life, without your personal mind's interpretation of what is good for them. This allows you to act in unconditional love by not judging the outcome, or about your client's life; you are acting with professional detachment in a position of unconditional love. It is at this point that you can introduce prayer if you so choose. Again the whole process is to focus your intention on the healing process without attachment to outcome.

Connect with the Reiki Universal Life Energy: Connect to Reiki in the way that you learned by using your intention to turn the Reiki on. Alternatively you can hold your hands with the palms facing each other until you can feel a flow of Reiki or else you can just put your hands on your clients shoulders, relax and intend Reiki and allow the process to begin. I know a lot of people who stand with the hands still in the prayer position and remind themselves of this strong connection to Reiki through their crown and feel the energy flowing down through their crown to their Dantein, the solar plexus and their hands filling with energy. You can introduce your own spiritual prayer or ask for help from enlightened beings to assist you with the healing session. There is no correct way so please use whatever works for you.

The treatment itself: Start with your hands on your client's shoulders for about five minutes to stabilize their energy with your own and start the flow of Reiki energy. You can then simply follow the hand positions as shown in the illustrations on pages 78-84. To complete the treatment it is a good idea to treat the knees and the feet as learnt on the VIDEO.

You can use a combination of traditional hand positions with aura scanning to establish if any area of the client is in greater need of the Reiki energy. Refer to the page on aura scanning.

Smoothing down the aura to finish: Make a number of sweeps over the recipient's body from their crown to their feet with your hands about four inches above the body to smooth down the client's aura to settle their energy down to complete their treatment. Make a final sweep from the feet back up the body to the top of the head. This makes sure the energy is flowing up the meridians in the correct way.

Disconnect from the Reiki energy to finish the treatment: You can shake your hands and then rub your hands together and say to yourself, "Reiki off". At this point some people like to offer a quiet thank you for the Reiki healing energy that they and their client have received. By doing this you are showing respect and gratitude.

Some Useful Treatment Guidelines

- Before starting the treatment check your own body hygiene.
- Wash your hands before and after giving a Reiki treatment if you can.
- Suggest that your client takes off their shoes, jewellery, glasses, watch and loosens their clothes if needed.
- Both of your legs and your client's legs should be uncrossed. It is understood that crossing the legs inhibits the proper flow of energy through the body's meridian system.
- Make sure your client is warm and comfortable on the treatment table. You might consider keeping a blanket handy and you can place a pillow under the person's knees to support the lower back and a pillow to support the head.
- Place your hands on the client slowly and gently and remove them in the same way. Keep your hands still when holding each position otherwise it would be distracting to your client.
- Keep your fingers together as much as you can but do not make your hands ache in the process.
- When your hands are over the client's face be careful not press on their eyelids or against their nostrils.
- When working on the client's head be careful not to breathe on their face.
- When working on the client's neck take care not to let the weight of your hands rest on their throat.
- When working over any sexual area of your client do not make physical contact. Let Reiki flow from a hands off position of about three inches above the body.
- Do not lean on your client or apply undue pressure. This is Reiki not massage!
- Do not try to force the outcome, just allow the energy flow; avoid giving your own personal energy.

The Full Reiki Treatment

Starting on a chair – Calming and settling your client

Note: These two starting positions on a chair only need to be included for the first treatment a person receives. Once a person has experienced Reiki you can by-pass this section and start directly face down on the couch.

1. Both hands on client's shoulders sending Reiki down their body into their Heart Chakra.

This position settles the client while opening the Aura to receive the Reiki Healing treatment.

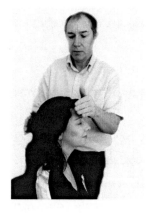

2. One hand is cupping the back of the client's head while the other hand is resting on their forehead over their third eye.

This position calms the client's mind and emotions. This will help release any tension or fear and soothe any headache.

The treatment continues on the couch – Client Face Down

In this position the client tends to feel more protected and secure able to let go more easily of tensions, thoughts and feelings. This prepares them to receive the final stage of the Reiki healing treatment to take place at a deeper level when they turn over onto their back.

1. Place hands in the T position over the neck and down the spine.

This position balances the spinal column working on nerves to arms, neck and shoulders increasing relaxation. Helpful in easing stress, this is a tension spot for computer workers.

Brings blocked emotions into your consciousness. Strengthens the throat chakra promoting self-mastery, self confidence and self expression.

2. Lay hands across the shoulder blades

(just above the bra line)

Treats the shoulders, upper back, heart and lungs.

This position is over the heart chakra and helps open the emotional body to unconditional love.

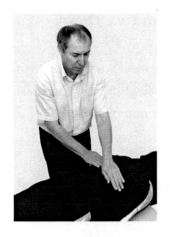

3. Lay hands across the mid back
(just below the bra line)

Treats kidneys, adrenal glands and the nervous system. Good position to help detoxify the body, treat allergies, hypoglycaemia and emotional shock. Helps with letting go of the past and releases fear. Treats the solar plexus chakra.

4. Lay hands across lower back at hip level.

Relieves sciatica, lower back pain and eases hip problems. Strengthens the nerves and lymph system. This sends energy to the sacral chakra supporting creativity and sexuality.

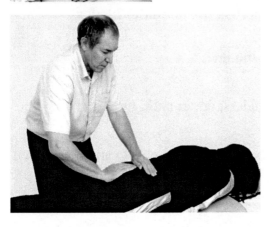

5. Place hands in the T position.

Balances sacral and coccyx problems. Sends energy through the length of spine stimulating the spinal cord and nerves, helps to realign vertebrae. This position is sending energy to the base chakra and helps with personal security; problems with existence. It is grounding and centring bringing a sense of security which is the perfect feeling to assist trust in the allowance of the Reiki energy when the client turns over onto their back.

The treatment continues on the couch - Client Face Up

Treating the front of the body deepens the whole healing process in the treatment. The client will have been totally relaxed through previously treating their back; this enables the Reiki energy to be received instantly you put your hands on their face.

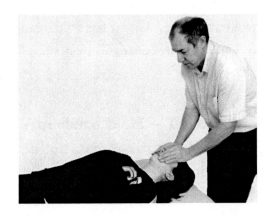

1. EYES - Lay your hands lightly on the right and left of the nose, covering the forehead, eyes and cheeks.

Balances the pituitary and pineal glands. Treats eyes and turns your consciousness to inner self, easing the whole body. Promotes relaxation

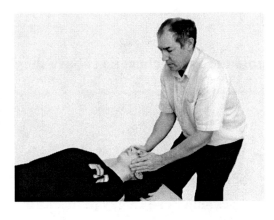

2.   TEMPLES Lay hands over temples, with your palms following the shape of the head, so that your fingertips touch the outside edges of the cheekbones.

This position balances the left and right side of the mind and body. It helps to ease stress, slows down racing thoughts and worries and assists with learning and concentration. Good for colds.

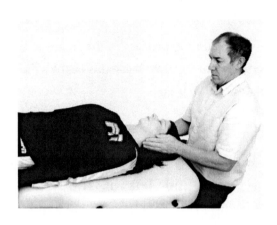

3. EARS – Place your hands so that the centres of your palms are over the ears. This position is good for treating problems with the outer and inner ear, eases symptoms such as noise or tinnitus, disorders of the throat and nose. Good for colds and flu, worry, depression and hysteria.

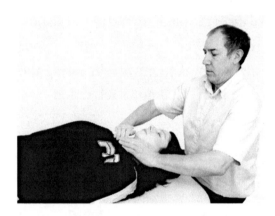

4. THROAT – Hold hands in V position above the throat, but do not touch it directly.
The throat chakra represents self-expression. When working on this position be very gentle and loving. Can help metabolic disorders, weight problems and low blood pressure.

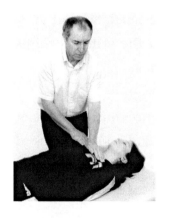

5. Lay hands across the upper chest just above the bra line.

Treats heart, lungs, liver, thymus gland.
Increases capacity for love, promoting acceptance and trust because you are sending Reiki energy to the heart chakra.

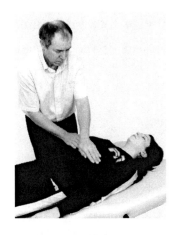

6. Place your hands across lower ribs just below the bra line.

This treats the liver, pancreas, gall bladder, stomach and parts of the intestine. It helps to ease hepatitis, gall stones, digestive and metabolic disorders detoxifying the body.
Balances the solar plexus chakra.

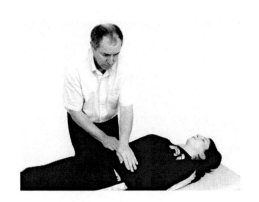

7. Place hands across the navel.

Treats eating disorders, digestive complaints, upper and lower colon and the bladder. Reiki is sent to the sacral chakra which is about lower emotions or passion, creativity, sexuality and personal power.

8. The magic triangle. Remember to hover modestly with hands in V position.

Treats the base chakra which roots us to the physical world. Releases fear and anxiety. It is grounding and centring bringing a sense of personal security.

The legs and feet carry the whole weight of the body and problems with the legs, knees and feet can be symptomatic of a hesitation and fear of moving forward in life. Emotions are also stored in the upper and lower legs. Treatment of the legs can release blocked energy.

9. Place hands on both knees.

The knees are about releasing anxiety and fear about moving into the future, into the unknown. Helps release pride, stubborn ego and inflexibility. The Reiki energy will bring compassion and understanding to assist the individual.

10a Cup hands around one foot at a time.

Helps problems with the feet and ankles. Helps to ground the client. One of the key energy points which helps to bring about a deep relaxation to the whole body.

10b Place both hands under the soles of the feet at the same time.

You are sending Reiki energy back up the body to balance the full treatment. This has the effect of re-energising and grounding helping the client to come back to full awareness.

Full Reiki Treatment on a Chair

A. To prepare the client smooth down the aura from the back of the client

B. When you are a Reiki 2nd Degree practitioner, open the heart and the aura at the back of the client with a large Cho-Ku-Rei.

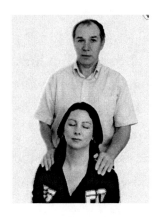

1. Place both hands on client's shoulders sending Reiki down their body into their Heart Chakra.

This position settles the client while opening the Aura to receive the Reiki Healing treatment.

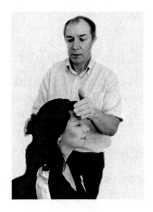

2. One hand is cupping the back of the client's head while the other hand is resting on their forehead over their Third Eye Chakra.

This position calms the client's mind and emotions. This will help release any tension and soothe any headache.

3.   One hand is held in front of the throat with the other hand being held at the back of the neck without touching the body.

This position treats the Throat Chakra
The effects and benefits are the same as described in the full Reiki Healing positions 1 face down and 4 face up.

4. Place both hands on the body above the bra line. One on the upper chest and one at shoulder level.

This position treats the Heart Chakra
The effects and benefits are the same as described in the full Reiki Healing positions 2 face down and 5 face up.

5.   Place both hands on the body below the bra line. One on the lower ribs and one level with the mid back.

This position treats the Solar Plexus Chakra
The effects and benefits are the same as described in the full Reiki Healing positions 3 face down and 6 face up.

6a.   Place both hands on the body in line with the navel. One on the lower back and one level with the navel.

This position treats the Sacral Chakra

The effects and benefits are the same as described in the full Reiki Healing positions 4 face down and 7 face up.

6b.   Place one hand at base of spine, fingers pointing down and the other hand on the knee closest to you. Then do the same again treating the other knee (changing sides if you prefer) as shown on our Video.

This position treats the Base Chakra
The effects and benefits are the same as described in the full Reiki Healing positions 5 face down and 8- 9 face up.

7.   Place both hands on the top of the feet at the same time.

You are sending Reiki energy back up the body to balance the full treatment. This has the effect of re-energising and grounding the client.

Reiki Exercise to Promote Well-Being

Whenever you feel stressed, unable to cope, overloaded, tense, tired, or worried it is worth taking the time to relax and make connection with yourself. Reiki healing energy can help you to relax your mind and body and to let go of tension more easily.

This exercise will balance you physically, emotionally and mentally. You can also use this exercise to treat other people.

Start this Reiki self treatment either sitting on a chair or lying down. Remain in each hand position for about three to five minutes. The total time to allow for this self treatment is about twenty-five minutes.

1.   Lie down comfortably or sit in a chair. Using your preferred method relax your breathing.

Close your eyes and place your cupped hands over them as you rest your palms on your cheeks.

This position balances the pituitary and pineal glands, which regulate hormones in the body that affect our emotional well-being. This promotes relaxation as it turns your awareness and energy back inside you.

2. Now place your hands on both sides of the top of your head, above your ears, touching the temples.

This position harmonizes both sides of the brain and has a relaxing and calming effect on the conscious mind. This improves clarity of thoughts, memory, eases depression promoting the enjoyment of life.

3. Now cup the back of your head with your hands, level with your ears and your fingers pointing upwards.

This position affects the unconscious mind and calms powerful emotions such as fear, worry, anxiety and shock. This will provide a feeling of security, helping to calm and clarify thinking.

4. Lay your hands on the left and right side of your upper chest, fingers touching just below the collarbone, just above the bra line. This position sends Reiki to the heart chakra.

When you feel depressed or emotionally low this position increases your capacity for love and openness to the enjoyment of life.

5. Place your hands behind you on your middle back at kidney height, fingers pointing towards the spine.

This position treats the adrenal glands plus the nervous system. It relaxes fears and shock, enhances confidence. By releasing fear we let go of the past, able to live in the present with joy.

Aura Scanning

This method is demonstrated on the free Healing Tutorial Video found on our website at www.new-awakening.co.uk.

When you receive your attunement to Reiki healing the energy centres in your hands are awakened and become very sensitive. With practice you will soon become aware of different energy sensations experienced when passing your hands over the aura of your client. You may experience tingling, a prickly feeling, warmth, coolness, pressure, a pulling or pushing energy feeling, pulsation or distortion of the energy field. These different sensations will show you where the focus of your Reiki healing needs to be and by scanning the whole aura you will gain a good idea of the areas which need to be worked on.

As you work within the client's aura you may intuitively detect information about your client or what is happening in their lives. I feel it is best not to share this information with the client as it can sometimes do more harm than good. What you say may have unexpected or harmful consequences; your interpretation could be incorrect. It is the ego's way of subtle superiority; 'I am the healer and know more than you'. Some people can be put off or become scared by the so called 'psychic stuff' that a therapist may have told them during a treatment. It is not necessarily for us to judge whether a client is in a position to hear certain information from us. Just trust that the Reiki energy will benefit them in the best way possible and for their highest good. You will discover that the client will often spontaneously talk about an issue that needs to be released, or be brought into their conscious awareness after the healing has occurred. In this situation the client has initiated the sharing and it is quite acceptable for you to share the impressions you received, if they are the same. In this way you validate your client's healing realisation. Always remember to respect the client and the process at all times as this is very special work.

First prepare yourself by asking to be shown which areas are most in need of treatment. To start the aura scanning, begin by placing your receptive hand about a foot above the crown of the person. Gradually move your hand to about three inches above the body and at this height slowly move your hand down the body over the face, torso and legs to the feet, noticing any energy changes previously mentioned. These changes may only be small but trust in what you are feeling and make a mental note of the areas that need special treatment. You may want to re-scan the aura at a different height above the body where you may notice different changes. Move your hand up and down slowly until you find the height which gives the most energy sensation, anywhere from several feet above the body to actually touching the body. Often the optimum height is three to four inches above the body.

When you find the place where the energy change can be felt most strongly stop and channel Reiki to that place with both hands, knowing that the Reiki energy will heal that place on a physical and emotional level. Keep treating the area until you feel the Reiki energy subside or you feel the area is complete and then rescan to check. Once you feel a change in the energy move on to the next place of energy imbalance, possibly making a mental note to return to the original place later. With practice you will be able to sense more easily the areas which need healing and in time you might find that you can sense just using your eyes. Continue like this until you have covered the whole body.

This process can take some time or it can be done more quickly at the beginning of a treatment or at the end to complete the session. It can also be the focus of the whole treatment if agreed with the client at the outset. You may agree to scan for a certain length of time and then continue with the treatment as usual.

Know that it is very good for the client to have their aura scanned in this way as health imbalances usually start in the aura and can be cleared before they have a chance to actually appear in the physical body. Also aura scanning can help the client to draw more Reiki energy into the areas of the body where it is needed, so scanning at the beginning of the treatment can be more beneficial. Please do not feel that it is absolutely necessary to follow this pattern however. The full Reiki treatment is complete in itself anyway.

Scanning your own Aura

When treating yourself with Reiki you will find it very useful to use the same aura scanning technique as outlined above, moving your hands through your aura to detect any energy changes. You may find you need healing in new areas you didn't expect and aspects of yourself that you were not aware of may be brought into your consciousness. When you meet an area of imbalance ask yourself kindly what happened to cause it and what you might do in addition to Reiki to help heal it. As the Reiki flows allow different feelings to be experienced freely and give them space to be healed without judgement. Allow yourself to love yourself. This process can make us more sensitive to our own needs, those of others and to the world we live in and it increases our sensitivity and so aids our own spiritual growth.

This can become an additional dimension for you in receiving the intimate process of Reiki healing for yourself. This process can make you aware of your deeper needs; it increases your sensitivity to yourself and others. You discover a greater connection with the world around you and notice that this deeper self-healing facilitates personal growth.

Meditations and Self Help Exercises

BREATHING MEDITATION

Breathing exercise to induce the Alpha state

Deep breathing from the diaphragm is the key to relaxation. A full deep breath increases the amount of oxygen as the body begins to function effectively, especially during mental activity.

To feel the full effect of correct breathing, place your hand over your navel and imagine you have a balloon in your stomach. Breathe deeply through the nose - as the balloon inflates your hand moves outwards. As you breathe out imagine the balloon deflating and feel the abdomen falling.

Before starting any exercise on relaxation always take three full deep breaths - and feel the tension and negative energy drain away on the out breath, breathing in positive energy on the in breath. Once you have learnt this breathing method to achieve meditation try using it with your Reiki Self Healing.

Here is the simple procedure

1. Imagine the balloon in your abdomen as this is where you transfer your consciousness. Breathe in relaxation and positive energy and hold the breath for three seconds.
2. Breathe out letting go of any tension and negative energy - feel the balloon deflate - and again hold the breath for three seconds. Become aware of the precise moment of stillness.
3. Breathe in again - be aware of the air filling your lungs - hold for three seconds.
4. Breathe out with a sigh - feel the air leaving your body. Hold for three seconds.
5. Breathe in - be aware of the air flowing in. Hold for three seconds.
6. Breathe out with a sigh and feel the tension draining away.

THE PRACTICE OF CHANTING 'I LOVE YOU'

Your main Goal in life should be 'Spiritual Awakening' which is a state of inner indestructible Happiness. You then discover that the limits in your life are only your own!

At the core of everyone - YOU and I and everyone else, we all want love. When you say or chant 'I Love You' as a mantra inside of yourself, you cleanse yourself of negative emotions and radiate at your core energy, which is LOVE.

You then RADIATE an energy that is common to us all and everyone feels it. The result is everything comes to you!

Chant or repeatedly say

'I Love You' 'I Love You' 'I Love You'

Repeat this mantra until you can feel a change inside of you

Use this mantra to Love your worries, problems, blocks, illness and they will transform into the Universal core energy of Unconditional Love. Mix this practice with the practice of Gratitude to increase its power. Connect with Reiki and start chanting the mantra to deepen your experience.

THE PRACTICE OF RESPECT

This very simple spiritual practice will bring amazing changes to your state of being.

Try it. Silently greet every person you meet 3 times with. "I deeply respect your life"

Try this even if you do not appreciate the other person. What you are doing is greeting their life as a spiritual being, on a level that is beyond judgement. You are raising your vibration to a new greeting of (The God in me recognizes and honours the God in you; Namaste). You will experience benefit as a result.

THE PRACTICE OF GRATITUDE

Gratitude and acknowledgement are essential components in attracting whatever you want in your life. Practicing gratitude eliminates personal dissatisfaction and complaining. This exercise will deepen the power, influence and effect of the exercise of chanting 'I LOVE YOU'.

Through the expression of gratitude on a daily basis you will create an even greater vibrational match for the future you want to create.

We recommend that you practice gratitude in the following way:

First take a deep breath, become centred so that you pay attention to your second sacral chakra (just below your belly button). This will bring focus and depth to what you are about to be grateful for.

Then say, with passion and emotional meaning, "I am grateful for ...." list as many as possible.

When you have finished this exercise just sit with as empty a mind as possible and notice how you feel emotionally.

The importance of keeping a Gratitude Journal

The importance of keeping the journal is that you can then go back and read from it and add new things to be grateful for. The journal will also reveal the spiritual growth of an individual as more human elements such as "I am grateful for my mother – I am grateful for my father – I am grateful for my boss" will emerge as a person develops more compassion, moving from things for me to social considerations.

CREATING A POSITIVE SELF-IMAGE

When you are experiencing negative feelings about yourself the following exercise will help you regain a positive self image of yourself. This will have a knock on effect of re-establishing your positive sense of self worth.

1. When you feel good about yourself your life condition will increase. What is happening? You are once again opening your heart to allow your higher loving self to transform your negative emotions into love. When you are really stuck and are unable to start this exercise because you feel so negative, use your Reiki healing to help lift you.

2. Imagine yourself as you would ideally like to be. Think about how you would look if you were as happy and confident as you wanted to be. How would you walk? What would you wear? What expressions are on your face? Where do you go? Take as much time as you need to see how you look when you are confident and full of self-esteem.

3. When you know what you will look like, make a little movie clip in your imagination of yourself, happy, confident and self-assured.

4. Now, imagine stepping into yourself in that movie. See what you see, hear what you hear and feel the confidence of being there and enjoying being exactly how you want to be.

5. Imagine waking up tomorrow as your ideal self feeling this good and imagine the day going exactly as you want it to.

6. Start your Reiki energy and then using your imagination send the Reiki energy to the new you.

In order to get a maximum benefit from this technique, please use it daily for at least a week. Keep on using for longer up to 21 days, or as often as you want to.

DEVELOPING SELF LOVE AND APPRECIATION

This is another exercise that will help you to feel better about yourself. It will also have the effect of re-establishing your self-respect and self-love. Whenever you are feeling low, depressed or are self-doubting it is your cherished friends and family who can see your strengths and values when you cannot. They will offer you affection, acceptance, appreciation and most importantly Love. When you see yourself as they can see you, your thoughts and feelings about yourself will transform into Self-Love.

1. Take several deep breaths to centre you and close your eyes. For about five minutes use the breathing meditation whilst at the same time also give yourself Reiki healing. Hold one hand over your heart chakra and the other hand over your solar plexus chakra.
2. Now think of someone who loves or deeply appreciates you. Remember how they look and imagine that they are standing in front of you.
3. Imagine stepping out of your body and into the body of the person who loves you. See through their eyes, hear through their ears and feel their love and good feelings as they look at you.
4. Notice in detail what it is that they appreciate about you. Finally understand these amazing qualities that perhaps you haven't appreciated about yourself until now. Take a few moments to feel good as you look at yourself.
5. Notice where the feeling is the strongest and give it a colour.
6. Imagine spreading that colour all through you, up to the top of your head and down to the tips of your toes.
7. Now double its intensity and brightness deepening the energy in your imagination.
8. As you open your eyes keep that feeling glowing inside you.

You can keep that inner feeling with you for hours and hours and repeat this exercise whenever you want to boost it. The more you do it, the easier it becomes and eventually it becomes automatic to love and feel loved.

The Dalai Lama apparently cried when he discovered that Western people had difficulty in loving themselves because from his Buddhist culture the idea of loving yourself is part of their conditioning.

THE LAUGHING BUDDHA

Hotei was a wandering monk who went around and took the sadness from people of this world. Due to his large protruding stomach and his smile, he is known as the Laughing Buddha. In China, he is dubbed the Loving or Friendly One. His image graces many temples, restaurants and amulets. Hotei has become a deity of contentment and abundance. Hotei shows us the power of laughter to transform our attitude towards life. He used it as a spiritual practice for himself and other people and it worked!

Laughter has more importance in transforming us than we realise; try feeling miserable when you are laughing. Today there are Laughter Therapists to lift people with depression and help transform the negative emotions that cause illness. People have just become well through the practice of laughter.

In our lives we tend to get caught up, stuck in the troubles and problems of everyday life at the expense of the beautiful richness contained within us; the higher self waiting to lift us into love to experience the sheer joy of existence.

Laughter is infectious - Become like Hotei then more homes will be full of laughter, dancing and singing. Lose your seriousness and you will become more healthy and whole. Enjoy this simple, fun exercise. I promise you it really does work. Your laughter will spread; it will become infectious so that tidal waves of laughter will spread everywhere. Your laughter will bring a gift of such joy and celebration to everyone. Explore it, enjoy it, most of all lighten up and have fun.

THE NATURAL WORLD

THE HEALING POWER OF FLOWERS AND TREES

There is an unbounded unrestricted state of being that is pure potentiality. This state excludes nothing. Your body may have limitations, your mind may have limitations, but your spirit, your Divine self has no limitations.

The Magical is about to Manifest
Your Real Being is Spirit   Pure Potentiality

In order to activate this law of Pure Potentiality, the realm of pure spirit, your true self, you have to get in touch with it.   HOW DO YOU DO THIS? The traditional way is by meditation, however because the general social consciousness of today's era tends to be very dense and quite heavy, sitting in meditation becomes very difficult for most people to practice to be able to obtain the stillness required. This approach also does not easily fit into most people's busy daily lives.

Meditation is a state of dropping your barriers and turning inwards but most people absorb from the outside. They tend to pick up on the general dense environmental awareness which is painful as they are unable to lift the heaviness from their aura (energy field) and turn inwards as intended. This is why Reiki works so effectively as it puts you instantly back in touch with your Divine Spirit and in turn activates your real true being of pure potentiality.

Spiritual methods of Divine connection that are very effective today are in the practice of chanting and through intimacy with Nature using Reiki Healing. To spend time in the natural environment, in a forest, up a mountain, on the moors, in a secluded spot all by yourself in solitude you will connect with the pure unbounded spirit because that same spirit is also there. When you get into this solitary experience with nature, you will feel the presence. When you have found a solitary place in nature activate your Reiki. Chanting the mystic mantra will strengthen this Reiki connection; you will learn these mantras on the Second Degree course. Then just become still and observe the flowers, notice as you become one with them that they are automatically sending you a healing vibration.

Record this experience in your journal. At first you may not notice much and different people will experience different messages, experiences and process the information they perceive in preferred different ways, because we are all unique.

For you it may be an instant experience but please be patient. If this is not the situation I promise you will experience this union, this connection and once you have achieved this experience, nature becomes magical; it will display a new found pulsating beauty to you. Once you have experienced this connection with flowers try trees etc.

I remember in the late 1980's when I was working in London I was fortunate to be able to go to Regents Park in my lunch break. It was there that I used this method to refresh myself with the magic of its plants and flowers. In this state moral judgement does not exist.

For now enjoy yourself with the Universal Divine Consciousness gift of life energy to us all and discover the hidden beauty within nature.

Appendix

Book and Music Source

The music of Deva Premal and Miten
www.mitendevapremal.com or www.prabhumusic.net

Cygnus Books (www.cygnus-books.co.uk)
Freepost (SS1193), Llangadog, Carmarthenshire, SA19 9ZZ

Gaia Books Ltd. London
www.Gaiabooks.com

Reiki Magazine International
www.ReikiMagazine.com

Body & Mind Music CD Store
www.bluewatermusic.net

New World Music
www.newworldmusic.com

www.soundtravels.co.uk   Music for relaxation, healing, chant and dance

Amazon Books CDs & DVDs
www.amazon.com

Websites

Spirituality - New Awakening   www.new-awakening.co.uk
Sports Psychology – Into The Zone   www.into-thezone.co.uk

Acknowledgments

I offer gratitude and appreciation to all my spiritual teachers, masters, friends, family and for their support and encouragement. Without the experience of meeting everyone in my life to date I would have never been able to have written this course. Thank you very much from the bottom of my heart to everyone I have ever met.

The following great people have helped me develop in knowledge, love and wisdom:

Osho – Bhagwan Shree Rajneesh, Amma and Bhagwan – oneness movement, Deepak Chopra, Eckhart Tolle, Virginia Satir – family therapist and last but not least Deva Premal and Miten for their mystically uplifting music.

Reiki First Degree Track Guide - Tutorial Audio MP3 – 2 Album Set

Reiki 1st Degree   CD 1   69 min

1	New Awakening Introduction	5.05
2	The Attunement	5.43
3	About Healing	6.29
4	Reiki History	7.09
5	Self Healing	14.14
6	Healing Others	10.45
7	Aura Scanning	9.31
8	The Chakras Affirmations	3.39
9	Your 21 day Journal	6.05

Reiki 1st Degree   CD 2   66 min

10	Reiki Music 'Universal Light' with 3 minute bells	

MP3 downloads available from our website at www.new-awakening.co.uk

My gift to you, a spiritual resource for the world

I have provided FREE OF CHARGE part two of your course which is the Attunement. I have also supplied FREE OF CHARGE three tutorial Videos which show you how to give Reiki Healing treatments on a couch, on a chair and how to scan the aura. Please go to our website at **www.new-awakening.co.uk** to view these videos as often as you like.

There are no restrictions as to how many times you can view these videos.

How to use the Reiki 1st Degree Distant Attunement Video

1. Watch the VIDEO all the way through on your own, in a place where you won't be interrupted, to get the gist of what is going to happen. Unplug the phone etc.
2. To feel a deeper experience continue by relaxing your state of mind by doing the Breathing Meditation listed at the back of this manual. This will prepare you to attune yourself more effectively.
3. Then replay the Video again from the beginning, this time taking 3 deep breaths, centre your awareness in your sacral chakra, moving your energy down from your mind. Relax and close your eyes. Now imagine that it is you sitting in the chair receiving the attunement.
4. When instructions are given, this is when I will now be talking to you and guiding you through the attunement. Following the sequence you can either do the instructed actions physically or see yourself doing them in your imagination.

Reiki Certificate of Training

Students who have studied the New Awakening Reiki System of Spiritual development qualify for a certificate of attainment. To obtain your certificate go to our website at:

www.new-awakening.co.uk   Then select 'spirituality' to see the log in area 'certificates'

You will need to log into the page: User name: **certificate**   Password: **certificate**

The Complete New Awakening Spiritual System

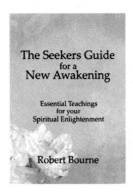

The Seekers Guide for a New Awakening

Essential Teachings for Your Spiritual Enlightenment

The Excellent You – How to get what you really want
Love and Relationships – Creating loving meaningful relationships
The Gateway to Enlightenment – Awakening to Universal Laws
Home Study Material Available
The Seekers Guide, Audio Course 6 CDs plus a Meditation CD
Includes Free Spiritual Attunements ISBN 978-0-9561159-7-3

Reiki Healing First Degree
New Awakening System

**This Home Study Multimedia Course is all about
Healing Yourself, Family, Friends, Pets and Plants**
Home Study Material Available
Course Manual, Reiki Music CD, Tutorial Audio Course CDs
Includes Free Spiritual Attunements ISBN 978-0-9561159-4-2

Reiki Healing Second Degree
New Awakening System

**This Home Study Multimedia Course Teaches
Three Sacred Reiki Symbols for
Physical, Emotional, Mental & Spiritual Distant Healing**
Home Study Material Available
Course Manual, Reiki Music CD, Tutorial Audio Course CD set
Includes Free Spiritual Attunements ISBN 978-0-9561159-5-9

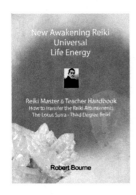

The Reiki Master – Teacher
New Awakening System

This Home Study Multimedia Course Teaches
The Reiki Masters Symbol and Divine Wisdom
How to Teach Reiki & Transfer the Spiritual Attunements
Home Study Material Available
Course Book Manual, Tutorial Audio Course CD set
Includes Free Spiritual Attunements ISBN 978-0-9561159-2-8

The 'New Awakening' method has a compassionate methodical approach through providing proven energy experiences which build upon each other creating a solid safe foundation for the student. This compassionate system created for the individual will enable the next spiritual opening to naturally occur safely. 'New Awakening' will support you with Divine Wisdom, Healing and Unconditional Love.

The 'New Awakening' system also provides three wisdom based companion personal and spiritual home study courses, with tutorial CDs, to support the seven spiritual openings. These courses are available as MP3 downloads – please view our website for where you can download them from. 'The Seekers Guide for a New Awakening' supporting courses are 'The Excellent You', 'Love and Relationships' and 'The Gateway to Enlightenment'.

When the CDs are listened to repeatedly, they have a transformative effect upon the consciousness of the listener. The 'Ah Ha' moments just keep coming over and over again. What could not be understood through reading alone becomes an enlightenment experience as the change in consciousness occurs at the soul level of awareness within you.

New Awakening teaches The Universal Life Healing Energy in three stages; Reiki 1st Degree, Reiki 2nd Degree, Reiki Master/Reiki Master Teacher, with each stage consisting of two parts, the first part is the professional home study multimedia course learning material. The second part is the practical 'Self Attunement' energy experience, that is provided free of charge, as our gift to you from our website. (www.new-awakening.co.uk)

About the Author

Robert Bourne is a Reiki Master Teacher, healer, author, resource manager for organisations and a spiritual course creator. He began his career in sports psychology, psychotherapy, hypnosis and NLP gaining an honours degree for his thesis on Auto-suggestion in 1986. In 1995 Spiritual fusion was experienced with the Beloved Universal Divine Consciousness revealing Robert's true mission as a spiritual teacher.

Robert was the founder of Reikiparty International, which was a friendship organisation uniting like-minded people. The Spiritual Organisation flowered in the spirit of Unconditional Love, whereby individuals who wished to unite with like minded friends were encouraged to do so by contacting each other with the view of helping and supporting each other on their spiritual journey. Reikiparty quickly evolved into a less structured organisation promoting the expanded spiritual system 'New Awakening'. This new spiritual holistic system is the compassionate flowering of the crown chakra within spiritual development. The organisation offers love, healing and friendship, providing guidance and encouragement for individuals who wish to hold fun events expressing the joy of Life. Because of the understanding that total freedom for the individual's personal expression of the Divine experience is embraced, no specific structure has been created as to how to hold events or support meetings. New Awakening supports those individuals who wish to make contact with other like minded friends in the form of providing 'how to do' free of charge downloads. You can find these free downloads from within our resource centre on our website at www.new-awakening.co.uk.

The expanded idea of the Reiki Healing Universal Life Energy being practiced for personal and spiritual development is now promoted to everyone. Reiki healing is seen as the first step to a greater energy experience of Unconditional Love to take place within the individual; to achieve an experience of bliss and Truth in the form of Divine wisdom and oneness enlightenment.

It was in 2008 that the phenomenon of New-Awakening was created. This is an advanced energy training based upon an Unconditional Love energy transfer. The place where no conflict arises is the consciousness of Oneness, of Unity consciousness. It is this consciousness that is the foundation of this new people's organisation. It is this place where you will arrive through studying all four courses in this total system for spiritual enlightenment.

Robert, author and course creator for Naturally You Publishing, is currently living in Devon in the UK. Robert's life's purpose is to offer teachings and energy experiences to bring about a change in higher consciousness for the individual. The creation of value is always the first consideration when creating interactive courses. The vision is to create a golden age wherein society becomes a loving spiritual experience for the whole of mankind.

Finally Robert would like to share with you

"I am devoted to sharing the blissful
Divine connection of purity with you"

Namaste

Caution and guidelines for your safety with Reiki

The exercises, hand positions and meditations described in this course manual are intended for the healing and harmonization of you as a holistic being. The course creator wishes to point out that, in the case of illness, a doctor or healing practitioner should always be consulted. The Reiki positions and meditations described may naturally be applied as an additional form of treatment. Reiki does not take the place of conventional medicine. Always consult your doctor for an acute or infectious condition and any problem of urgent concern.

Reiki is a complementary therapy that works effectively alongside orthodox and alternative health-care solutions.

Lightning Source UK Ltd.
Milton Keynes UK
14 February 2011

167502UK00005B/42/P